52

WEEKS

OF

FAVOR

WISDOM DECIDES YOUR LEVEL OF FAVOR

Dr. Jerry A. Grillo, Jr.

"For you, O Lord, will bless the righteous; with favor you will surround him as with a shield." Psalm 5:12

FZM Publishing

Copyright 2006
By Fogzone Ministries
P.O. Box 3707 Hickory, NC. 28603

ISBN 978-1-4276-2963-0

Printed in the United States of America.

Table of Content

Preface

Favor is one of God's greatest gifts to us. Favor can open seasons that by all rights should be closed to us. Favor makes no sense!

Everybody is eligible for FAVOR... but not everyone will qualify. Both Ruth and Orpah, in the Book of Ruth, were eligible for the blessing... They were both tied to the same city and crisis... both lost their husbands... both were connected to the same mentor, Naomi. Both were eligible; only one qualified. I am a firm believer that we must work the requirements of being favored.

There has to be a balance in our thinking. Favor isn't some tool we can use and abuse to get people to shout or sow. *Favor is a gift!* Favor is the one ingredient that works void of human intervention. Favor is simply someone liking you enough to help you walk into your next season. Get ready for a season of favor to explode in your life.

I've taken the time to put on paper what I believe, will help you walk in favor and also walk in a daily lifestyle of Kingdom connection. This book is written in such a way that you can read it through like a regular book, or you can take a chapter a week and make it a weekly devotional. Let me encourage you to take your time and do a chapter a week. Let the next 52 weeks become your year of favor.

I promise, in a few days you will begin to experience an incredible season of Favor!

Dr. Jerry Grillo, Jr.

Week One

THE SOURCE
OF GOD'S FAVOR

Favor isn't some new theology that we have created in this century. Many are teaching and preaching on the word "favor". The truth is that *favor* was preached way before you and I were speaking about it. The man that started the ministry of *favor* was Zerubbabel in Zechariah 4:7. God instructed Zerubbabel to rebuild the temple, a job that was going to be impossible in the natural; not by power, or by might, but by God's Spirit. Zerubbabel was instructed to go out every day and speak to the capstone; GRACE, GRACE! FAVOR, FAVOR!

Speak to the end of a thing, not to the beginning. Favor is the power to move out of your present, into your future and accomplish the task, or vision, by faith and not by might. If you want to walk in favor you must gain **WISDOM!** It takes wisdom to understand timing and faith and how to walk in a season of revelation.

Caution! Revelation without wisdom is divisive. Many people today are seeking information, with all kinds of self-help books and television programs on "how to" and "what not to do". People are gaining knowledge faster than they can process it.

Information without wisdom and understanding is dangerous.
This is how the enemy is destroying our churches. We are seeking the process and function of things instead of the **source**. We begin to weed out the non-favored when we understand the source of favor. I don't want to hang out with anyone who hasn't been favored by God. The source of favor is wisdom; the understanding of time, so you can know how to move and use favor. Today, in your time with the Holy Spirit, I challenge you, not to seek favor, but the **wisdom** of God. Ask the Holy Spirit to give you understanding and help you recognize the season you are walking in. When you develop a clear understanding of your season you will possess the knowledge to operate accordingly in that season. Revelation isn't healthy if you are not operating and possessing the power of wisdom. Revelation without wisdom is divisive.

FACTS ABOUT WISDOM:

WISDOM WILL EXCEL YOU TOWARD YOUR GREATNESS... *"And God gave Solomon wisdom and understanding exceeding much, and largeness of heart, even as the sand that is on the seashore. And Solomon's wisdom excelled the wisdom of all the children of the east country, and all the wisdom of Egypt. For he was wiser than all men"* 1 Kings 4:29-31

WISDOM ATTRACTS THE RIGHT PEOPLE..."And there came of all people to hear the Wisdom of Solomon, from all kings of the earth, which had heard of his wisdom."* 1 Kings 4:34

GOD USED WISDOM TO DESIGN THE EARTH... *"How many are your works, O LORD! In wisdom you made them all; the earth is full of your creatures."* Psalm 104:24 NIV

THE RIGHTEOUS SPEAK WORDS OF WISDOM... *"The mouth of the righteous man utters wisdom, and his tongue speaks what is just. The law of his God is in his heart; his feet do not slip."* Psalm 37:30-31 NIV

SPENDING TIME WITH THE HOLY SPIRIT PRODUCES DIVINE WISDOM... *"Surely you desire truth in the inner parts; you teach me wisdom in the inmost place."* Psalm 51:6 NIV

THE WISE FEAR THE LORD, AND GAIN KNOWLEDGE... *"The fear of the LORD is the beginning of knowledge, but fools despise wisdom and discipline."* Proverbs 1:7 NIV

WISDOM IS BUILT ON UNDERSTANDING... *"Get wisdom, get understanding."* Proverbs 4:5 NIV

WISDOM DOESN'T COME WITHOUT A PRICE... *"Wisdom is supreme; therefore get wisdom. Though it cost all you have, get understanding."* Proverbs 4:7 NIV

THE ONLY PROBLEM YOU HAVE IN LIFE IS A WISDOM PROBLEM...

WISDOM DETERMINES YOUR LEVEL OF FAVOR...

THE WORD OF GOD IS THE WISDOM OF GOD...

Week Two

THE REASON FOR FAVOR

FAVOR IS ACCESS...

"*Jesus Christ, through whom we have gained **access** by faith into this grace in which we now stand. And we rejoice in the hope of the glory of God. Not only so, but we also rejoice in our sufferings, because we know that suffering produces perseverance; perseverance, character; and character, hope. And hope does not disappoint us, because God has poured out his love into our hearts by the Holy Spirit, whom he has given us.*" Romans 5:1-5 NIV

*"For through him we both have **access** to the Father by one Spirit."* Ephesians 2:18 NIV

"In him and through faith in him we may **approach** God with freedom and confidence." Ephesians 3:12-13 NIV

Favor is not being supplied with the abundance of worldly wealth and riches. Favor is not a great job, or a promotion. Favor is not large ministries, or large houses. One of the greatest weaknesses in the American church is that we have a tendency to make every focus, **a focus of self-promotion and self-advancement**. You have missed the real reason for favor if you believe prosperity is about having and getting. It is about being and becoming!

FAVOR IS THE TRANSFER OF ACCESS, NOTHING MORE AND NOTHING LESS.

In our daily verses we read that Jesus Christ through whom we have gained access by faith into this grace (favor) in which we now stand... For through Him we have access to the Father by one Spirit. God has favored us through Jesus Christ; that favor, by the blood of Jesus, gives us access to something much greater than money, fame, or promotion. It allows us the privilege to enter into what was once forbidden and secretive. This access is the greatest gift given to men. We are now allowed to enter as many times as we want into God's presence.

This is the greatest gift to humanity. Access to God's presence can create everything we will ever need and everything we have ever wanted. This holy place is reserved for those who have confessed Jesus as Lord and Savior. Those who are walking according to God's Word... Our focus should be Him (Jesus), and we should pursue God's perfect will for our lives daily.

- God doesn't respond to our cries...
- God doesn't respond to our needs...
- Pain and discomfort do not get His attention...

WHEN YOUR NEEDS CONTROL YOU THEN YOU ARE OUT OF CONTROL.

If needs alone attracted the favor of God then why are there so many innocent children dying of hunger and pain in this world?

The truth is that God is moved by your pursuit of Him. Pursuing God moves God toward you, and even better, moves you closer to Him. When your heart is focused on pleasing the Father (God) then you are allowed access to Him through Jesus.

The Word of God plainly says in Matthew 7:7 *"Seek God and we will find God. Knock and the door will be opened."* God is not hiding; He is not playing a childhood game of hide- n-seek. God is giving us a clue to what gets His attention and when we choose to seek, look and search for Him, then we will find Him. When we find Him, we will find His **FAVOR**... Favor is Access!

ACCESS IN HIS PRESENCE PRODUCES WISDOM...

You have access to His presence and in His presence there are doorways to your destiny and purpose. Favor is the ability to enter and learn about Him, so you can learn from Him. My mentor and spiritual Father, Dr Mike Murdock, says, **"The difference between seasons is an instruction."** I want to add a second part to this. *"The difference between instructions is information."*

We lack the necessary resources when we lack the proper information to succeed. God is the author of life, so wouldn't it be beneficial for us to seek Him first? Why don't you go to a mechanic when you're having heart problems? The mechanic lacks the knowledge to fix what's hurting you. This mentality works for every area of life except in the church. Stop discussing your pain with those who are unqualified to solve it.

Knowledge is power... absolute power is absolute knowledge. God is all-knowing. The theological word is **omniscient**... which means *all-knowing*. When we are in pursuit of God we are actually in pursuit of absolute knowledge; absolute knowledge gives us absolute power! Could it be, the reason so many are powerless in so many situations, is that they lack the knowledge that could excel them to the next season? If this is true, stop looking for God in all the wrong places and start looking for Him in you. Seek Him today and you are going to find Him.

It's not what you know that's hurting you; it's what you don't know. Hosea 3:6 says, *"My people are destroyed for lack of knowledge."*

WHEN WE UNLOCK THE KINGDOM WE UNLOCK FAVOR, and in return, we increase in all things... income, wealth, health and life. Spend the next few minutes meditating on these verses. Ask the Holy Spirit to reveal to you the plan and purpose of God. Seek the Lord today! Worship while you wait.

Lord, make my life count. I want to be highly favored. I am willing to pay the price for favor. I confess that my future is secure because my present is in Your will. In Jesus name Amen.

Week Three

THE PRICE OF FAVOR

THE PRICE OF FAVOR IS TIME

"He shall speak pompous words against the Most High, shall persecute the saints of the Most High, and shall intend to change times and law." Daniel 7:25 NKJV

Time is the only gift God has given us that we can choose to use, or waste. Think about it! You didn't decide your parents... You didn't decide your race... You didn't decide what country you would live in. The only real decision you make everyday is what you will do with your time. You can waste it, or use it. When you choose a career, you have to decide on how much your time is worth. In reality, you're not just paid for the job you do, you're actually paid for your time.

People go to work everyday and work eight to ten hours of their best time of the day for a paycheck at the end of the week. They sold their time for money. Now, everything else in their day is surrounded by their willingness to make a trade off of their time. Want your kids to know you better? It will cost you time. Want your wife to be closer to you? It will cost you time. The real gift of life is the gift of time! Time is a coin. You can spend it anyway you wish, but you can only spend it once.

Satan shall speak pompous words against the Most High. Pompous means *self important, arrogant.* Satan comes in with arrogant words that cause us to focus on him and not the Lord. His intent is to rob us from the laws and timings of God. When we become so focused on the world and its system, we begin to self-exalt. The enemy keeps us blinded to real truth, and the lack of truth causes us to miss the timing of our blessings. Time represents seasons! Seasons are not governed by the clock, or the calendar; they are governed by *revelation and truth.*

What you feed will grow. Man is made up of three parts! Body, soul and spirit; what you feed will grow. The body feeds on food. The soul, or your emotions, feed on feelings; your spirit feeds on truth. **The food for the spirit is truth**!

The principles of God, which are His laws, are the keys that promote us to our success. Satan's task is to keep us **self-motivated and self-absorbed**, and in that process we miss everything the Lord has planned for our lives.

Problems become our focus... money... a career. These things can grab your focus and begin to steal valuable and precious time.

DR. MIKE MURDOCK SAYS, "THE PROOF OF RESPECT IS TIME."

How can we really express ourselves to someone if we don't spend time with them? The same is true with God. How can we say we love Him and respect Him, if we continue to go each day without spending any time with Him?

We need to understand that **TIME IS THE PRICE OF FAVOR.**
* **Reaping a harvest takes time…**
* **Building a career takes time…**
* **Falling in love takes time…**

Learn to wait with the proper expectation. Give God time to work out your greatness. If we desire to have the favor of God in our lives we are going to have to stop doing so much for ourselves and take some time and spend it with Him. The enemy is working hard to overload your life. Do what so many are unwilling to do… take the time necessary to get to know God.

Make this your prayer today; that you will slow down and notice the good things in life encoded in the moment.

Pray this today:

Lord, help me, not to be so self-absorbed and self-motivated that I walk past those things that I should notice; such as birds singing, children playing, trees and flowers growing, and people who matter.

Lord, give me the power to walk away from those decisions that are costing me the time necessary to spend with You and those I love. Lord, I want to notice You and extract Your love and graciousness in every moment of my life.

In the name of Jesus! AMEN.

Week Four

WHAT HAS GOD PLACED IN YOUR DAY?

"Do not be in a hurry to leave the king's presence."
Ecclesiastes 8:2-3 NIV

"You expected much, but see, it turned out to be little. What you brought home, I blew away. Why? Declares the LORD Almighty! Because of my house, which remains a ruin, while each of you is <u>busy</u> with his own house?" Haggai 1:9

SLOW DOWN... TAKE IN THE JOURNEY

- *Hurry is the enemy to accuracy...*
- *Hurry is the enemy to excellence...*

Joy is the reward for discerning and distinguishing a divine deposit in a moment. Frustration is trying to extract from the moment what hasn't been deposited in it yet. I can't go to my bank and make a withdrawal if I haven't made a deposit that can cover that withdrawal. If a person writes a check for an amount that exceeds what's been deposited, the bank sends that check back as 'insufficient funds'. It's called a "bounced check".

The same is true with relationships. You will miss making the daily deposits of joy, peace and love if you let life's success keep you in a constant hurry. You will discover that you have "insufficient funds" when you go to write those "checks" with your family, friends, or co-workers. You've been bounced! This is the greatest curse in our society.

WE ARE TOO BUSY TO STOP AND NOTICE ANYTHING GOOD.

Why is it we spend so much time chasing success only to find ourselves empty and void of the peace we have labored so hard to possess?

I placed this devotion right after the subject on time because I believe that it is easy to forget what we meditated on yesterday. I want to create a sense of urgency that we are **too busy**! Stop missing what's been deposited in a moment. Time is costing you your joy.

YOU'RE TOO BUSY:

- *When you can't take a day off.*
- *When you can't stop and notice the birds, the flowers and the awesome things that God paints daily for your enjoyment.*
- *When you leave before your children get up and get home after they're in bed. **You're too busy!***
- *When you have to make Sunday the only day for your yard work and chores. In doing so, you sacrifice the gathering of God's people.*

- *When you haven't taken your wife out of town in a long time.*
- *When you can't even stop long enough to enjoy what your success has already accomplished.*
- *When you look around and your babies are now teenagers, and you didn't even notice until the house became empty.*
- *When your children have to make an appointment to see you.*
- *When your wife has to ask for permission to enter your atmosphere. Stop the insanity!*

When was the last time you took the time necessary to enjoy the success you have already obtained? The Lord was clear in His word about remembering the Sabbath and keeping it holy. At one time, we gave honor to the day of rest in this country. Stores weren't open; people would sit on their porches and watch the day go by. They took the Sabbath and made it holy. Holy, means there must be a day in your week that is different. Even God, who is omnipotent (all powerful), had to take a day off and rest from His labor...

"And on the seventh day God ended his work which he had made; and he rested on the seventh day from all his work which he had made. And God blessed the seventh day, and sanctified it: because that in it he had rested from all his work which God created and made." Genesis 2:2-3

The Hebrew word for *"rested"* is *Sabbath (shaw-bath'); primitive roots; to repose, i.e. desist from exertion; used in many implied relations (causative, figurative or specific).*

Are you missing the joy of your day? The little things that would cause great peace and great joy are not encoded in your daily success, but in the smile of your children, or the kiss of your wife good-bye for the day. It is little moments that create great joys in your life. Don't let these moment in life pass you by.

Take A Time-Out!

When a player calls a "time-out" they are saying we need a moment to gather our thoughts. Games are lost when coaches fail to use their time-outs. You need a break when everything around you is causing you to lose the game of life. *Call a time-out!* You will start to gain perspective and control of your day.

Week Five

THE POWER OF FAVOR

THE POWER OF FAVOR IS PURPOSE!

Today, you're going to gain the understanding that everybody has a purpose. Many live life and never know their purpose.

Why are you here? Why did God allow you to live through the things that others have died in? There must be a greater reason for your life than to get up everyday, go to work, pay your bills, raise your family and then die. I need to believe that there is a greater purpose for my life than just existing. How about you?

Many people never sit down and write a goal for their life. You will never discover your purpose if you ignore the need to create some goals and dreams for your life. Your purpose will surface when you develop a plan to succeed and just stop taking up space. The world is full of people who possess the greatness to accomplish anything they desire. They could lift the bar of life to higher heights. Instead, they keep accepting their life; staying at some hourly job, paying their monthly bills and crying about their boring and mundane life, but never doing anything about it.

"YOU CAN'T CHANGE WHAT YOU ACCEPT OR TOLERATE."

I know pastors who hate their church. They have cried to me that they can't stand how their people act and respond to the truth; how the people are angered when they try to teach them how to escape their prison of ignorance.

When I confronted a certain pastor about making changes his response was, "*Well, they are good people.*" I replied, "So! Hell is full of good people." Anyone who doesn't want to change when God's truth is being preached has a hint of ungodliness in them. What we have in churches like that is a bunch of '**good ungodly people**'. This pastor has settled... He has become comfortable with a good paycheck and has lost the power of what his real purpose is. **"YOU CAN'T CHANGE WHAT YOU TOLERATE."**

I call this living life in a **"RUT"**. A *rut* is formed when others have driven down a dirt road and left their tracks. When those tracks dry it makes it difficult for anyone to drive on that road unless they stay in the same tracks as the others. When you haven't set any goals for your life, and you never discover your purpose, you will find yourself living a life that someone else has dictated to you. Stuck in a rut! The only thing different between a rut and a grave is the dirt in your face. Don't be afraid to think outside the box. Get up and start dreaming! What would you do if money weren't an option?

TAKE THE TIME TO DREAM... Set a goal for your life so your purpose will surface. The power of favor is purpose. The dictionary defines *"purpose" as, the object for which something exists, or is done; end in view.*

Purpose is stronger than adversity. I've heard numerous stories of how men in crisis stayed alive because they had purpose. Knowing that you have a purpose gives life more meaning... makes life more valuable... get a mind-set of wanting to accomplish what you've been purposed for. God has a plan for your life. Sit down and take the time to discover the real reason you are here.

Your assignment is waiting to be revealed. You must understand that you can't create your destiny...you can only discover it. The Holy Spirit designed you... He knows your assignment!

When I was moving from one building to another at the church that I founded, The Favor Center; the building I was looking at was three times bigger than the one we were moving out of. I was squashed when I walked through this enormous building and began to add up the extra cost of making this new building a reality. In my mind, there was no way we could afford to move; yet, we needed to move. We had outgrown the building we were meeting in, and I knew that if something didn't change soon we would start backing up. However, after sitting down with the landlord, I was horrified!

Fear rose up so fast in my mind that I left the meeting completely defeated. Walking into my apartment, I went straight to my bedroom, shut the door and just sat there totally defeated. I could feel depression setting in on me. I was reading a book at that time by Dr. Mike Murdock, "31 Reasons People Don't Have Financial Harvest".

Though Dr. Murdock and I had never met, I had bought the book in a local bookstore. Opening the book where I had left off, I began to read and what I read blew my mind! *"Double your vision; get a dream that is bigger than you... A dream, a vision that you cannot afford and God will get involved in it."* There was a sudden surge of faith that shot up in my heart the moment I read those words I began to cry and laugh at the same time.

Something in my spirit jumped; those words had put purpose back into my life. I began to see the bigger picture. Purpose gave me the faith to press on. Within six months I was standing in my new building, looking at the new carpet, the bigger platform and smelling the new paint. Tears began to flow out of my eyes looking around at what purpose had accomplished.

All of a sudden I was startled by my wife... she said, "Don't you need to be leaving to go pick up Dr. Murdock from the airport?" That's right; I had called him the next day after I read those life-changing words, and He agreed to come and dedicate my new sanctuary. See how powerful purpose is? Don't let another day go by without writing your goals and a vision that will force your purpose to surface.

YOU WERE CREATED TO ACCOMPLISH SOMETHING FOR GOD'S KINGDOM

Discover your purpose... Discover the opportunities that are tied to your purpose. You were created to walk in a life of incredible favor.

FACTS ABOUT PURPOSE:
- *Purpose creates focus.*
- *Purpose creates vision.*
- *Purpose promotes passion.*
- *Purpose demoralizes fear.*
- *Purpose will push you when others have deserted you.*

Week Six

ENVY,
THE PROOF OF FAVOR

"FAVOR NEVER ENTERS YOUR LIFE ALONE"

When you begin to discover that God has favored you, get ready for those around you to become jealous and envious of your access.

"Now Israel loved Joseph more than all his children, because he was the son of his old age: and he made him a coat of many colors. And when his brethren saw that their father loved him more than all his brethren, they hated him, and could not speak peaceably unto him." Genesis 37:3-4

Joseph's brothers were so envious of him. They hated Joseph when Jacob gave him his coat of favor. They didn't hate him because he had dreams, and they didn't hate him because he was the youngest; they hated him *because he was favored.*

ACCESS OF FAVOR PRODUCES PROMOTION...

Remember, when you are favored, you are given access to people that have the potential to promote you to your next season. When great leaders begin to favor you, get ready. Those who are not allowed your access will become angry with you. They will try to crowd in on your favor.

Don't share your favor with others when you are allowed special access into great peoples lives. Bishop T.D. Jakes says, "Favor isn't fair."

ATTITUDE OF FAVOR CREATES SEASONS OF FAVOR...

Joseph's ability to maintain a favored heart, even when his circumstances were saying something totally different, kept him blessed.

Look at his journey, and you will discover that struggle is the birthing ground for greater potential.

First, he was captured by his brothers and thrown into a well. You may be wondering how that was a good thing? Mind you, they were plotting to kill him. The enemy is trying to kill you; if God has to put you in a well to keep you alive, so be it. As long as there is breath there is hope for a better outcome.

Although they threw Joseph in a pit! He was favored in the pit.

Joseph kept his attitude of favor in spite of the enemy's attack.

FAVOR CAN REVERSE THE CURSE...

To add to Joseph's dilemma, he was sold into slavery to an Ishmaelite. Now remember, Ishmael was the flesh seed of

Abraham. He represents the cursed side of our lives. Here's the power of favor. God will reverse the curse and have the curse that was scheduled to defeat you, deliver you from your pit! (Genesis 37:27)

Joseph was sold to an Egyptian man named Potiphar.

"And the LORD was with Joseph, and he was a prosperous man; and he was in the house of his master the Egyptian." Genesis 39:2

God was with Joseph. No matter where he was placed, whether by crisis, or promotion, people noticed that God favored him.

"And his master saw that the LORD was with him, and that the LORD made all that he did to prosper in his hand. And Joseph found grace in his sight, and he served him: and he made him overseer over his house and that entire he had he put into his hand." Genesis 39:3-4

Joseph maintained a favored attitude in promotion, and when there was a problem of false accusation, he had to maintain his countenance.

YOU MUST PASS THE TEST TO BE HIGHLY FAVORED...

While Joseph was growing prosperous, Potiphar's wife began to lust after Joseph, and she set a trap for him. While Potiphar was gone, she cornered Joseph in her bedroom and tried to seduce him. Now, I can't imagine that Joseph wasn't tempted. I believe he was, but I also believe that he weighed out his favor versus spending the night with Potiphar's wife. He just wasn't quite convinced that he should trade his favor for a night of pleasure. So what does he do? He runs away.

A GOOD RUN IS BETTER THAN A BAD STAND...

Potiphar's wife accuses him of the very thing he ran from. She lied about him and his character. False accusation is usually the last step to supernatural promotion; you must maintain the right point of view, the right attitude. (Genesis 39:6-19) Your point of view is always determined by your "viewpoint".

Potiphar's heart was kindled with anger when he came home and heard what his wife had to say about Joseph; so, he put Joseph in prison, but not just any prison, the King's prison. If you were going to be sent to any prison this was the one to be sent to. Joseph was now a man in prison.

What did he do? How did he respond? You guessed it. He kept an attitude of favor. Now, he's favored in the prison. Remember, this all started when his brothers became envious... when his father favored him. Envy always follows favor.

PRISON TO PRAISE HIM...

Joseph was in prison, but he was not alone. The Lord was with him in the prison. Joseph maintained an attitude of favor in the prison. After awhile, he was promoted in prison, and then one day, the highest man in Egypt sent for him. When it was all said and done, Joseph became favored in the palace and was promoted to second man in all of Egypt. It all started with someone favoring him and others becoming envious of him.

His father favored Joseph; his brothers got angry and plotted to destroy him.

- *Joseph kept an attitude of favor in the pit...*
- *Joseph kept an attitude of favor in a problem...*
- *Joseph kept an attitude of favor in false accusation...*
- *Joseph kept an attitude of favor in prison...*
- *Joseph became favored in the palace...*

Praise God for trouble! Trouble is the doorway to your promotion. Get ready for favor when you see people around you getting angry at your access and increase.

Week Seven

A THANKFUL HEART IS A FAVORED HEART

"In every thing give thanks: for this is the will of God in Christ Jesus concerning you. Quench not the Spirit..."
1 Thessalonians 5:18-19

"And let the peace of God rule in your hearts, to the which, also ye are called in one body; and be ye thankful."
Colossians 3:15

THE UNHOLY ARE ALWAYS UNTHANKFUL...

Walk in a spirit of gratitude. Learn to be grateful for your life. The Word of God says that we are to give thanks in everything, for this is the will of God. This isn't to say that you should be thankful about bad situations, but it does mean to maintain an attitude of thankfulness. You can go through bad things and still keep your joy by finding something good in the bad situation. An unthankful person has the atmosphere of a complainer, and that kind of spirit will quench the Holy Spirit.

Don't let situations and circumstances in life keep your heart from seeing the good in everything.

MAKE GOD FEEL GOOD ABOUT BEING GOD!

An attitude of gratefulness... being thankful... giving praise continuously in your life creates an atmosphere of joy in the presence of God. I want God to feel good about being God.

If you were to extract precious metals from the earth, say gold for instance, you would have to dig, or pan through a whole lot of dirt to find one ounce of gold; yet, when you uncover that one ounce of gold, it would be worth more than the pounds of dirt you had to remove to find it.

Learn to extract the gold out of every situation to maintain a life of thankfulness. Okay, maybe your teenager came home late and missed their curfew. Thank God they came home, others had to go to the hospital and identify their child's body that night. Sure, life isn't always going to lead you through a path of roses and honey, and if it did, you would still have to deal with thorns and bees. Develop an attitude of gratitude.

THANKFULNESS REPLENISHES THE ATMOSPHERE FOR MIRACLES TO MULTIPLY...

When Jesus was on His way to heal Jairus' daughter, the woman with the issue of blood was also in pursuit of Jesus' anointing. When she reached Him first, and touched Him in faith, Jesus' anointing was drained. Virtue flowed from Him into her, and she was immediately made well. Now, Jesus stopped in a crowd of people and requested knowledge of the one who had touched Him? Why? She had pulled from Him His virtue and He needed to be thanked and praised for the atmosphere to be replenished for the next miracle (Luke chapter 8). When she stood, she said, "It is I" and then she thanked Him. Jesus was able to go to His next assignment full and replenished.

A thankful heart keeps the atmosphere replenished for

miracles to happen. Just a thought! Could it be the reason we are not seeing more miracles in our churches, is because there aren't many thankful people present? What have you already complained about today?

THANKFULNESS CREATES AN ENVIRONMENT WHERE GOD IS REWARDED...

"Enter into his gates with thanksgiving, and into his courts with praise: be thankful unto him, and bless his name. For the LORD is good; his mercy is everlasting; and his truth endureth to all generations." Psalm 100:4-5

- *The proof of character is gratitude...*
- *The proof of gratitude is change...*
- *The proof of change is progress...*
- *The proof of progress will be problems...*

Problems will always produce promotion, and promotions will create a season of increase. The process to your increase starts with an attitude of gratitude.

THE FAVOR OF GOD FOLLOWS A THANKFUL HEART...

God loves those who understand how to be thankful over little things. God will begin placing big things in your life when you learn the secret of being thankful for the little things that happen around you. Don't let another day slip by that you don't find something to be thankful for.

"Because that, when they knew God, they glorified him not as God, neither were thankful; but became vain in their imaginations, and their foolish heart was darkened. Professing themselves to be wise, they became fools." Romans 1:21-22

DON'T BE FOOLISH... BE THANKFUL FOR TODAY!

Week Eight

HOW TO RECEIVE FAVOR

I've heard, as you probably have, that it's better to give than to receive. Though this statement is true in the standpoint of your harvest being much greater than your giving, it is also good to be a receiver. Let's not act "holier than thou". Receiving is GOOD! I like it when people give me things. Who doesn't? When you are a giver who keeps on giving, it's nice when someone decides to give to you. I love to receive gifts. Let's be honest, we all like to have someone bless us. Let me give you a scripture that we all should know.

"Give, and it shall be given unto you; good measure, pressed down, and shaken together, and running over, <u>shall men</u> give into your bosom. For with the same measure that ye meet withal it shall be measured to you again." Luke 6:38

How is God going to bring you a financial return? Through men who are blessed around you... He's using other obedient people to give it back to you. Your ability to sow creates the power for God to open the door for a Boaz to enter your life.

YOU WILL LOSE ACCESS TO A GIVER WHEN YOU LACK THE UNDERSTANDING OF HOW TO RECEIVE...

We spend so much time preaching the seed message that we forget to teach the receiving message. Years ago, I was in need of a new car. My old car had had it, and I was tired of driving a car that kept breaking down. So, I went to the car dealership, but while I was there, I began to hear the voice of the Lord in my spirit telling me to leave. There was a particular car that I had in mind, but when the dealership got through with me, it was obvious that I was about to put myself in worse financial debt.

DEBT IS AN ATTEMPT TO BE SOMETHING YOU ARE NOT.

The only way they were going to get me into this car was by putting me in payments for the next six years. I wanted that car so badly! When the salesman went to talk to his manager, once again, I heard that still voice, "You're settling, wait on me..." I knew it was the Holy Spirit, so I left. I was so upset and disappointed. The drive home was about thirty minutes. I could sense in my spirit that the Lord was testing me. He wanted to see how I would respond to Him and what my attitude would be. This happened twice! A few months later, I was sitting down with a businessman discussing my need for a car. Just a few short days later, this same businessman, who worked for a Mercedes dealership, bought me a car. I drove off the lot with a C280 Black Mercedes.

I was so messed up I couldn't sleep that night. I was horrified! My humility couldn't handle such a big gift. I called him the next day, took him to breakfast, slid the keys across the table and said, "Here, I can't take this car; it's too big a gift." He slid the keys back across the table and asked, "How can you believe God to favor you with big things if you can't receive them?"

I learned that day that it's much harder to receive than to give!

I asked Him what he wanted from me. He said, "How about 'thank you'?" "That's it?" I asked "Yes, that's it! Just be thankful."

KEYS TO BEING A GOOD RECEIVER:

1. *Never receive a gift from someone, and lay it aside and say,* *"You're more important to me than that gift."* That gift was a part of them! You just made their gift a small thing.
2. *Never trivialize someone's gift*...Make every gift matter. A small gift could be a test for a greater and bigger gift. No matter what I buy my daughter, she always says. *"It's what I've always wanted."* She makes me feel good about giving her a gift.
3. *Make every gift important*... When you're receiving many gifts it's easy to start noticing only the big ones, stay focused and make every gift count...
4. *Thank people properly*... always take time to read their card first. Don't rush what someone has written. They spent their time trying to document their feelings.
5. *Encourage those who give.* Be happy about your gift no matter what it is.

"A gift is as a precious stone in the eyes of him that hath it: whithersoever it turneth, it prospereth." Proverbs 17:8

"As for every man to whom God has given riches and wealth, and given him power to eat of it, to receive his heritage and rejoice in his labor-this is the gift of God." Ecclesiastes 5:19-20 NKJV

"... And you shall receive the gift of the Holy Spirit. For the promise is to you and to your children, and to all who are afar off, as many as the Lord our God will call." Acts 2:38-39 NKJV

God is a giver. You will never see God taking. He is always giving. You are the receiver! Just because you are asked to sow seed doesn't mean that you're not still on the receiving end. When God impresses your heart to sow, it's not the seed He has on His mind, it's your harvest. Thus, even in sowing, you are sowing to receive. God is the *Lord of the Harvest! We are lords of the seed!* When we do what we are supposed to... release what we are responsible to release... it allows God to be Lord over our harvest. We must learn to be good receivers.

Pray this prayer today.

Lord, help me today, to become a good receiver. I'm sowing my seeds, but help me get ready to receive my harvest. Give me the strength to always keep the right attitude when receiving. AMEN.

Week Nine

GETTING VS. RECEIVING

THERE'S A DIFFERENCE BETWEEN GETTING AND RECEIVING!

I was sitting on my couch one night and saw this Christian advertisement that I didn't like. It was some guy standing on the edge of a bridge; getting ready to bungee jump. He forgot to make sure his cord was tied off when he jumped ... with this big thump you hear him groan. The caption comes up. **GOT JESUS! GET HIM!** This just didn't sit right in my spirit because there's a difference between *getting* something and *receiving* something.

If I mail a package to your house and the mail carrier delivers it to your address, in their opinion, you have gotten your package. They don't know if you're opening the package, or someone else, but if I call them to inquire, they will say, "Yes, they got it". However, if I hand you a package personally, and you take it from my hand, you didn't get it, you received it. If the court needs to get legal papers into your hand, they will send them through a Sheriff and he will personally put them in your hand. Why? Because they want to know that you have personally received them. They're not relying on you getting them; they are making sure you have received them. They even have you sign your name to prove you have taken those papers from the Sheriff's hand and received them into yours.

YOU CAN'T GET TRUTH; YOU MUST RECEIVE TRUTH...

Truth isn't something someone is teaching. Truth is something you're catching. You catch the truth by receiving it. That's the difference between hearing and learning. Just because you are hearing something doesn't mean you are learning it.

Many sit in a classroom daily while a teacher speaks about different subjects; but few leave enlightened to the truth of what was being taught.

Why? Not everyone in that class has a desire to learn. Some are sitting there trying to satisfy a grade, but others, are there to increase their knowledge.

To receive something, you must come into agreement with the person that is trying to give it to you.

"But as many as received him, to them gave he power to become the sons of God, even to them that believe on his name." John 1:12

You have to come into agreement with God to receive His Son, and this gives you the right to become one of God's children. You are not in line for your inheritance until you are in the order of sonship. You're not in "sonship" until you receive JESUS!

"For if by one man's offence death reigned by one; much more they which receive abundance of grace and of the gift of righteousness shall reign in life by one, Jesus Christ" Romans 5:17

*"For ye have need of patience, that, after ye have done the will of God, ye might **receive the promise.**"* Hebrews 10:36

When you receive this information you have to be willing to agree to it. When you're getting something, you can disregard it afterwards. How many times has someone given you something that you turned around and gave away when they left? You only got their gift, but when someone hands you something that you take, use, and feel the loss when it is gone, then you have received that gift.

Many sit in church week after week, coming to get something that they are unwilling to use, and they sit and wonder why they are not increasing. These kinds of people never get involved. They just want someone to hand them something without trying to do what it takes to receive it. To leave your church, or the presence of God changed, you must receive the truth no matter how much it hurts. Make the effort from now on to be a receiver and not just a hearer. I close with this. James said to be a doer of God's word and not just a hearer. Hearers are *getting* it and doers are *receiving* it.

Lord, help me to be a receiver of Your will and Your words and not just a hearer. I'm not getting it; I'm receiving it! In Jesus Name, AMEN!

Week Ten

GET POSITIONED
FOR AN OUTPOURING

Do you desire to be favored? Wouldn't you like to be in a place where the devil has no access to you? There is a place in God where Hell cannot get to you. You must be in the right position to be able to find this place, and you must have the right posture.

- **Being saved doesn't mean you're going to be blessed.**
- **Being saved doesn't guarantee you will walk in wisdom.**
- **Being saved doesn't bring you healing.**
- **Being saved doesn't mean you are walking in the fullness of the Holy Spirit.**

There is a position that you can walk in that will open up the Kingdom's best for you to experience.

"And every plant of the field before it was in the earth, and every herb of the field before it grew: for the LORD God had not caused it to rain upon the earth, and there was not a man to till the ground. But there went up a mist from the earth, and watered the whole face of the ground." Genesis 2:5-6

It had not rained on the earth after creation; God couldn't release the full potential of rain because He lacked one main ingredient for an outpouring. He needed a man in position to till the soil.

POSITION IS IMPORTANT! God wouldn't open heaven and bring a fresh outpouring of rain. God needed a man to till the soil. God waited for a man to be in position… Think about what this implies. God couldn't release all of heaven's resources because He didn't have a person who would do the work after it rained.

God releases enough substance to keep the earth supplied in order to survive, but not enough to flourish. A mist would show up and keep the earth moist. Now, don't despise the mist of God. The mist is always the first stage of God's presence. The mist was doing the job of maintaining the earth. The earth could survive a long time just on the mist.

You and I can live a long time with the mist of His presence. Many Christians are living on a mist! They are living on just enough of God to keep them in church, but not enough, to break them totally free from the bondage of their past. Many are bound by things that they were promised freedom from. They are simply living on the mist.

The mist will only maintain our lives; there's not enough left over to cause an increase of abundance. A favored life can't live on a mist; it needs an outpouring! God can't open heaven until someone is in position for heaven to be opened. Let me ask you a question. If God has been doing what He's been doing in your life with a mist, what could you be walking in if you ever got in the position for an outpouring?

WOW! Think about that for a moment! What could you be missing just because you are not willing to do what it takes to get in the right position?

What could you be experiencing if there was an outpouring of God's rain in your life today? That's my prayer for you today. I want you to discover what your assignment is so you can be where you are suppose to be; so you can stop experiencing the mist and start living under an outpouring.

God wants to open heaven! He's been waiting on you so He can bless you with heaven's best. What are you waiting on? Look up right now and ask the Holy Spirit to teach you the right posture and position to receive.

"And it shall come to pass afterward, that I will pour out my spirit upon all flesh; and your sons and your daughters shall prophesy, your old men shall dream dreams, your young men shall see visions: And also upon the servants and upon the handmaids in those days will I pour out my spirit." Joel 2:28-29

POSTURE IS IMPORTANT...
MANNERS ARE NECESSARY....

I was walking with my son one day, and as we were walking, I became irritated with the way he was walking. He was slumped over; dragging his feet, making that annoying sound with his heels scrubbing the ground. I spoke up and said, *"Pick up your feet, stand up and look like you know who you are."* Later that night while we were eating a meal, again, I became irritated watching him eat. He was eating as if he hadn't eaten a meal in five years. He was smacking! He was slumped over as if he were about to drown in his plate. As his father I said, *"Sit up, and bring your food to your mouth, not your mouth to your food. Quit smacking. It's rude!"*

He looked at me and said, "Dad, why are you always

watching what I'm doing? How come I have to?" **You know the rest**! I looked at him as this sense of pride shot up in me, and I could feel the spirit of all fathers of times past overtake me. My reply was so profound... **"Because I said so..."**

That night I was awakened by a noise, and while I was trying to go back to sleep, the Lord began to speak to my spirit. He impressed on me that what I said to my son was incorrect. Manners are important.

You see, I'm his father, and he doesn't have to act any certain way to stay in my atmosphere. He doesn't have to have manners to eat with me. He doesn't have to stand up and have good posture for me to love him and want to provide for him. We teach our children manners, not for us, but for the people they will be in front of when we are not with them. I want my son to be accepted in other people's atmosphere. I want him to know how to act at someone else's house, or table. So, I teach him the proper posture and position so others will notice him in a positive way.

TEN FACTS ABOUT POSTURE:
1. Your Posture determines how others will see you...
2. Your Posture lets others know what you think about yourself...
3. Good Posture promotes confidence...
4. Good Posture proves you like who you are...
5. Good Posture gives others a sense of security when they are around you...
6. How you Posture yourself in God's presence will determine if you get God's attention...
7. A Posture of praise and worship are the only keys to His court...
8. Posture is the result of good training...
9. Good Posture proves you are disciplined in how you treat your body...
10. Good Posture is healthy for your bones to grow properly...

Let's get in position for an outpouring.

GODLY POSTURES:
Posture of faith...
Posture of love...
Posture of loyalty...
Posture of kindness...
Posture of sowing seeds...
Posture of not missing church...
Posture of tithing...
Posture of faithfulness...

Sit down and pray; see if you can write down some good spiritual postures that will help establish your position so you can live under an open heaven today.

This is strong; when you are in the right place you can experience the rains of heaven. You will live the rest of your life void of the fullness of heaven until you are positioned where you are supposed to be. You will only experience the power of religion; the mist of God.

I don't want you to miss out on what the Lord has for you. My greatest fear is to get finished with this life, enter heaven, and have the Lord take me to a warehouse of blessings and say to me, ***"This was all yours, but you wouldn't get in position for me to pour it on you."***

Take some time and make sure that you are where you are supposed to be. Wealth is scheduled to a certain place.

Week Eleven

DON'T LET YOUR CONDITION ROB YOU OF YOUR POSITION

The word *"condition"* means: *"anything that modifies or restricts the nature, existence, or occurrence of something else; external circumstance or factor, a manner or state of being."*

Is there a condition from your past that is robbing you from a proper posture in your present and stopping you from walking into your future?

DELIVERED BUT DAMAGED...

Your past will stop you from moving into your future if you haven't dealt with what has hurt you. Most of us, who are willing to be real, will confess that we all have a past.

Where you came from has no bearing to where you are going. Your past doesn't have to keep you from your future.

Today, we're going to understand that what we did cannot stop us from what we need to be doing. *Conditions* can be manifested in your present through many forms such as: Anger, bitterness, distrust, inability to express your emotions, fear of making changes, sexual disorders, bad attitudes, insecurity, inferiority, a controlling spirit, low self esteem, a critical spirit, exaggerations and embellishment, never being able to face the truth about your situations, or a judgmental spirit...

Here are some circumstances that may have hurt you, or wounded you in your past, that could be causing the list above to manifest in your life.

- *An abusive father or mother, who never expressed their love to you, but had no problem showing you anger in punishment.*
- *An unloving parent who was never there for you when you needed them.*
- *A father that was too busy; when you were making your way through school accomplishments he was never the face you saw in the audience.*
- *It may be that someone you trusted abused that trust and violated your space. This offense usually comes through sexual abuse...*
- *You may have experienced an abandoned childhood; your parent(s) left you and never tried to keep a relationship with you. This leaves you void, hollow and empty. An emptiness that no one can fill.*
- *You could have gone through some major sickness during childhood that caused you to be angry...you didn't get to do what others did.*

I could write for pages on the abuse that people have had to live through; emotional, physical, racial, financial, and spiritual. So much hurt goes unnoticed. Today is your day to release the pains of your past so you may take your position for your future.

There's a story in the Bible that I believe is a great message for people like us who have had conditions to overcome. I'm not this great man that was born great! I've had to climb high mountains to be where I am today.

I had Dyslexia, I was molested as a child, and I had a spirit of fear and low self-esteem. I went through a divorce at an early age of twenty-five, and that divorce was the result of all my screw-ups. So, when I tell you God can use you after a mess, believe it!

In First Samuel chapter nine, David takes his place as King after years of running from Saul. David, though he was God's choice, wasn't the rightful heir to the throne. Saul had a son named Jonathan, and Jonathan had a son named Mephibosheth. Mephibosheth, was dropped by someone he trusted when was a baby and both of his feet were broken. His feet never healed properly, and he grew up lame. His condition was brought on by someone's failure to carry him in a crisis. (2 Samuel 4:4)

David had one covenant that he hadn't yet fulfilled when he took the throne. He needed to do good to Jonathan's offspring. You see, David wouldn't have stayed alive long enough to be King had it not been for Saul's son, Jonathan, who stayed loyal to David. David paced the floor of the palace...pulling his hair and screaming, "Is there no one left in the house of Saul that I might show my kindness to?" (2 Samuel 9:3)Meanwhile, in the house of *Machir*, the son of *Ammiel* in the land of *Lo Debar* sits a man who...

- Should have been King...
- Would have been King...
- Could have been King...but was sitting in his *condition* in the place of obscurity.

These three names have powerful significance.

1. *Machir means slavery.*
2. *Ammiel means associates.*
3. *Lo Debar means dry place or obscurity*

CONDITIONS OF YOUR PAST WILL KEEP YOU IN SLAVERY TO THEM...

That's what your *condition* will do. It will place you in bondage to it. Mephibosheth is in bondage to his condition, enslaved to his injury. You will start looking for people who are hurting just like you when you start living with the limitation of your hurts. You will stay in slavery to your past, with those around you speaking only about your past.

Do you wonder why you find yourself all alone? No one wants to hang around someone who is always wounded; stuck in Lo Debar. This is what you can look forward to as long as you keep living in past hurts, mistakes and failures. Let me give you a deep word, *let go of your past!*

YOUR CONDITION WILL PLACE YOU WHERE NO ONE WILL NOTICE YOU...

David sends for Mephibosheth, not to mock him, not to laugh at him, or to kill him. He is driven by a love for Jonathan that now has him wanting to give back to someone in Jonathan's house. Mephibosheth is just like you and I. He's a type of the church. Jesus has a covenant that He's in need to fill, and we are the ones sitting in our condition needing a Savior.

They take this crippled man, wash off his dirt, put him in the King's garment, perfume his hair and body, take him out into the King's court and sit him in the floor. Now, he's sitting in the floor all cleaned up, but he still has a condition. He can't help himself to the table no matter how badly he wants to. All of a sudden, the door of David's chambers open and in walks the King!

Imagine what might have been going through Mephibosheth's mind. *"Here he comes; I know he brought me here just to make fun of me. He's going to embarrass me and then kill me. After all, it was my grandfather that drove him away and tried to kill him..."*

David, however, does the complete opposite of what Mephibosheth is thinking. David lowers himself to Mephibosheth's level. Isn't this just what Christ did? He left His throne and came down to our level.

Then David put his arms under Mephibosheth's legs and began to pick him up. Isn't this the way Mephibosheth received his condition; someone carrying him had dropped him? Now, he has to submit to the very thing that wounded him in the first place. He might be able to conquer his condition if he's willing to trust someone again.

HURTING PEOPLE USUALLY HANG OUT WITH THOSE WHO ARE HURTING...

Who dropped you? Who let you down when you needed them the most? Who has hurt you so badly that you have lived most of your life not trusting anyone with your heart? You will never be able to heal until you begin to trust again, love again, and believe in someone again.

You are about to be picked up off the floor of your hurts, your failures and your frustrations and be placed at the Kings table. David takes this young man over to his table and sits him right beside him. Mephibosheth is sitting at the table, still lame in both feet. No one knows what's wrong with him; as long as he stays at the table no one will notice that he has a condition.

Let me ask you something, why stay sitting in the floor of your condition when you could be sitting at the table in your spiritual position?

Love again, take another chance at a relationship, forgive that parent for hurting you, let go of the chains that are keeping you in your condition. Your healing is today!

Lord, I pray for those who are hurting reading this chapter. I ask You to begin to heal their heart. Lord, give them the peace that they have been seeking for. Open their hearts and heal their fears. Holy Spirit, let love flow in the areas they have shut up for so many years. Open those doors that have their secret hurts behind them. In Jesus name Amen!

Week Twelve

SURVIVING YOUR DARK SEASON

The process of seasons is one of the most misunderstood subjects in life. It never ceases to amaze me how many people in life don't try to figure out and understand what season they are in.

Dr. Mike Murdock told me that every season has a code of conduct, or protocol, in order to enter it. Your present season will remain permanent if you lack the knowledge of the code for the next season. This is devastating! Imagine never being able to leave the season you are in.

SATAN'S GOAL IS TO ROB YOU OF YOUR SEASONS...

One of the enemy's goals is to keep you from discovering your next season. He accomplishes this by keeping your focus on everything that is circumstantial, so you lack the ability to see the bigger picture.

"And God said, Let there be lights in the firmament of the heaven to divide the day from the night; and let them be for signs, and for seasons, and for days, and years." Genesis 1:14

Here is the first time we find the word *'seasons'* in the Bible. The word *'seasons'* in the Hebrew means "a fixed time, or an appointed time..." **Let's go deeper.**

First of all, we must understand that not all seasons are going to be good.

"I will bless the LORD, who hath given me counsel: my reins also instruct me in the night seasons." Psalm 16:7

Not all seasons are set up to live by the daylight of success. There are going to be dark seasons in your life. We must understand that without darkness there can be no light. Dark times must come for us to understand day time. We tend to become more productive in the daylight after we have survived the night. God will usually dispatch a blessing to you in your dark seasons. Weeping may endure for the night, but something's coming in the morning! When is the darkest part of night?
MIDNIGHT!

Have you ever stopped long enough to think that just when midnight strikes so does morning; your new day? Simultaneously, life dished out a dark season with your morning attached to it. Your joy is connected to that dark season.

Notice the next verse.

"I have set the LORD always before me: because he is at my right hand, I shall not be moved." Psalm 16:8

How does the psalmist tell us to respond to our dark seasons? Set the Lord always before you. When you can't see the light around you, trust in the light that is in you. Keep your perspective. Don't focus on the dark clouds! The sun still shines under every dark, stormy cloud. You can't see it because the storm has temporarily blocked your view. That doesn't change the fact that eventually the sun will shine again.

The same is true with dark and tested seasons. Make up your mind today that no matter how hard a season is, you will not be moved!

Next the psalmist says:

"Therefore my heart is glad, and my glory rejoiceth: my flesh also shall rest in hope." Psalm 16:9

In the midst of my night season, I will take a position of praise and keep my heart lifted. You must learn how to encourage yourself. Stop waiting on someone to call you with a word. Get up! Motivate yourself out of your night season. Praise until your heart is lifted and your spirit is rested in hope of a better day. You must learn that sometimes you aren't going to feel God, but you can praise God, and in praising Him, move Him into your night season. Understand verse 10... ***"For thou wilt not leave my soul in hell; neither wilt thou suffer thine Holy One to see corruption." KJV***

Learn how to survive your storm. Keep looking! In the midst of your dark season is the code, or key, to get you out. God has made a path in His presence.

MAINTAIN YOUR JOY IN JOYLESS SEASONS...

When you stay in the center of His presence, you start seeing the darkness as the platform for light to rule. There can be pleasure in your hard time because you understand the code of conduct in your dark season.

Now, you are opening the door to the next season. Read the last verse slowly.

"Thou wilt shew me the path of life: in thy presence is fulness of joy; at thy right hand there are pleasures for evermore." Psalm 16:11

A path means that someone, or something, has already walked through and worn down a place for others to follow. Don't you see? God has already been through your rough season and has carved out a path for you to follow. Many never discover the path simply because they refuse to stay in His presence.

You can only discover the way out if you have spent time with the truth (Jesus). *"For they shall know the truth, and the truth they know shall make them free."* There's a way out of every season. The way is encoded in the presence of God. How are you going to face the season you are in? With boldness and praise!

Today is your day to walk into a new season...

Week Thirteen

ENTERING YOUR NEW SEASON

"It's a new season, it's a new day... there's a fresh anointing and it's coming your way..." Israel Houghton

Today, we are going to go deeper and learn how to exit a season so that we may enter the next one properly. How you leave one season determines how you enter the next season. Today, many people are changing churches, yet still can't seem to get with it. They left their last season wrong, and they are hindered to connect in their next season. How about you? Are you a person who can't seem to stay connected in any God moving church?

Notice I said "God moving" because dead churches don't qualify. Did you leave talking about someone? Did you get mad and leave when you got offended instead of sitting down and doing what the word of God commands you to do?

You actually shut the door to being anointed in the next season when you left wrong. God will never take you past your last act of stupidity! (Just a thought)

You can enter God's presence stupid, but you will never leave stupid. Quit making excuses why you won't get involved; why you aren't growing spiritually. Stop blaming the preacher! Stop blaming your job! Stop blaming your family! Step up and repent! You will never open the door to your next season until you go back and make right what you did wrong.

Now, hold on! Don't get angry with me. By the way, if you're angry right now, then you're probably guilty. Don't shoot the messenger! I didn't say it, God did. I'm not trying to offend you. I'm trying to open the door to your next season...

- A season of power...
- A season of prosperity...
- A season of increase and anointing...

My goal is to open your heart for change. You matter to me dearly. That's why I'm writing this to you. You really do matter! I want you to discover your next season. When you move up, so does the Kingdom of God.

DISCOVERIES DECIDE SEASONS...

Every truth, good or bad, will change a season for you. Children live in a new season everyday because they are making new discoveries everyday. Adults hardly ever change their seasons because they rarely want to take the risk that children do to discover new things. Jesus said He would not receive you unless you come to Him as a little child. Could it be, that He meant unless you have the faith of a child, and are willing to do and try new things, He could not receive you?

You have become dead to life when you stop growing and changing. Don't live life behind the mundane of safety and security. Get out and try new things! Dream bigger! Plan bigger! Dare to make some new discoveries. Your new season is waiting on you.

THE DIFFERENCE BETWEEN SEASONS IS AN INSTRUCTION...

- When God wanted to change Noah's season He gave him an instruction... *"God told Noah to build Him an ark."*(Genesis 6:14)
- When God wanted to change Moses' season He gave him an instruction... *"Moses go and tell Pharaoh to let my people go..."* (Exodus 4:19)
- When God wanted to change Abraham's season He gave him an instruction... *"Abram get thee out of thy country..."* (Genesis 12:1)

"THE INSTRUCTION YOU'RE WILLING TO FOLLOW CREATES THE FUTURE YOU'RE ABLE TO WALK IN..."
(Dr. Mike Murdock)

Every season is tied to an instruction. There must be a man of God speaking into your life to go from your present season into your next season. Your wealth and increase is tied to a man of God. How many people have missed their new season by simply refusing the instruction of a man of God that has been placed over them?

How about you? Have you missed your next season because you've refused to be obedient to the Senior Pastor God has placed over you?

EVERY NEW SEASON HAS A CODE OF CONDUCT TO ENTER IT... If you refuse to learn what it takes to enter the next season, your present season will remain permanent. You will stay stuck in your present season without the voice of a spiritual father guiding you to your next season.

Elisha would have stayed permanently stuck behind the butt of an ox and a plow had God not sent Elijah to him.

If Elisha had not recognized the code of conduct and received Elijah, he would have stayed stuck in the rut of life.

Elisha had questions about his life that he was unable to answer. Elijah had an answer to a question in his life that forced him to seek out the one who was seeking change. Someone, right now, is looking for you to change your season. There is a Boaz who's been given the power to solve a problem you are going to face.

Increase, healing, and wealth, are all tied to a man of God who is scheduled to change your season. My life changed drastically when Dr. Mike Murdock spoke into me. I changed when I received his instructions. Every seasonal change in my ministry has been through the voice of someone that was above me speaking down into me. Let me make something clear. We not only learn what to do from those around us, but we also learn what not to do.

Today, ask the Lord to help you to be obedient to your senior mentors. Don't try to succeed without them. You may find money increasing in your life, but that doesn't mean that God is in approval of your lifestyle. You are open for attacks of the enemy without the covering of a corporate church. I want to increase in all areas of my life, but I don't want to increase void of my spiritual covering.

INSTRUCTIONS MAY SEEM IRRATIONAL BUT NOT IMPOSSIBLE...

God has a way of challenging your faith by requiring something that appears to be irrational in the natural. Every instruction from God is usually irrational, but not impossible; for instance, walking on water, raising someone who's been dead for four days, calling demons out of someone and feeding five thousand with five loaves and two fishes. God is always going to stretch you to a season that requires trusting Him. The proof of faith is when you can't understand it, but you move out into it anyway. Just follow God's instructions.

Let the Lord lead you today. Follow His instructions. Be obedient to the Holy Spirit, He has been given as a gift to guide us and teach us in all truths. We can live a life of bliss. We can walk in incredible healings. All we have to do is trust God and obey Him. Obedience is proof of trust.

Week Fourteen

NO WORSHIP NO RAIN!

Worship is acquisition…

"**W**orship with a more excellent worship and God will enter in a more excellent way."

"And it shall be, that whosoever will not come up of all the families of the earth unto Jerusalem to worship the King, the LORD of hosts, even upon them shall be no rain." Zechariah 14:17

If my people don't come up to worship Me, there will be no rain. No rain, no harvest; no rain, no growth. Heaven must be open for it to rain. Worship opens God's eyes toward you, and heaven will be open where God is looking.

If we understand the process of the outer court, then we know that anyone can praise God. Psalm 150 says, *"Let everything that has breath praise the Lord…"*

The outer court, or courtyard, was full of a mixture of races. Anyone, from Jews to Gentiles, was allowed to mingle in the courtyard of praise. You didn't have to be of their faith to praise with them. Let everything praise the Lord! Praise is what we usually like to do. People love the energy of shouting and the fast pace music. Even the worldly can sit in our churches and feel comfortable in praise. That's Okay! We need to begin the process of making our voice heard before we are allowed to step closer to the throne of God.

Sitting on the platform in our church gives me the ability while I am praising and worshipping, to also see others in their praise and worship. I notice those who are suffering a lifestyle of disobedience, anger, disloyalty, bitterness, etc., they can't worship. They can praise God...they shout, jump and are exuberant in the outer court, but the minute we open the doors to enter into the holy place, they seem to shut down.

Here's a favor key: *Movement toward God always reveals the weakness of man.*

People with issues drop their hands, stop singing and start looking around as if they are finished. This causes me to question, what in the world is going on? Then it dawned on me. Praise brings God into your atmosphere, but worship keeps Him there. Praise brings God in your presence, but worship brings you into God's presence. Having God enter your home, church, or anywhere you are, is awesome within itself, but to have God open the door for you to come into His presence is a whole new level of accountability and responsibility. Enoch was allowed the access to walk with God, and one day He walked with God and was not! (Genesis 5:24)

HOW TO MOVE IN GODLY PROTOCOL:
- *You must enter His gates with thanksgiving in your heart.*
- *You must enter His courts with praise.*
- *After you have passed these tests you can worship God. (Psalm 100:4)*

If you aren't thankful, you will never be able to praise God. If you can't praise God you will never be allowed to worship Him. **Be allowed**? Someone may ask. Yes, your lifestyle is the foundation to be able to worship Him. If you haven't dealt with your sins at the gate and left them there, you will not be allowed into the most Holy Place. Worship, is a privilege reserved for those who really love Him. "The proof of love is pursuit."

If you aren't willing to do what it takes to climb up to a higher place of worship, there will be no open heaven for you. Every week many come as close as they can to His Most Holy Place, but few desire to do what it takes to enter. I pray that today you are examining your lifestyle so that you can enter into real worship.

REAL WORSHIP IS UNREHEARSED.... Real worship isn't the time during your church service when the worship leader starts singing a song that moves you emotionally to respond. No sir! Real worshippers worship in their daily routine. They'll stop every now and then to offer up a word of acknowledgement, or worship to God.

WORSHIP IS THE GOLDEN CONNECTION TO GOD'S BEST.... I'm not trying to sound risqué, but a spirit of thankfulness and praise is only foreplay to the real deal. You can praise your spouse in the mall, at the store, and around your children, but you can't worship your spouse in the mall, at the store, or around your children.

You worship in the privacy of your secret chambers. That is where your seeds are transferred for your future. It's at the moment of real worship that you become bare, transparent and vulnerable.

The same is true with God. If we want God to make a seed transfer, we have to enter into His secret chamber reserved only for those who are willing to be bare, transparent and vulnerable. How about you; are you willing to be exposed? If so, then you're about to enter His presence. Those who are willing to leave carrying **His** seed of change and increase can enter. You can't enter if you aren't willing to become weighed down with His seed.

I'll never forget when my wife was pregnant with our first child. She may have become large in the natural, but she was glowing from head to toe. It was as if she was turned into another person. *She probably was.* She had a glow around her, a glow that indicated something was happening that men will never understand. She was carrying life within her. She had a seed, a child, which only two people could create when they come into agreement. Life was the result of our worship, our connection. The same is true when we worship God.

When someone sexually forces themselves on another person without consent, it is called rape. I'm not going to elaborate here, but I will say this, God is not going to come into our church services and rape us. He's not going to plant any seeds in us if we are not open to receive Him.

WORSHIP IS ACQUISITION... Which simply means that when you worship God, you acquisition Him to be released on your situation.

13 Reasons Why You Should Worship God

Worship releases the favor of God...
Worship will help you past the test... (Genesis 22:5)
Worship blocks problems... (Joshua 5:14)
Worship is proof of trust...
Worship produces prosperity... (Psalm 22:27-29)
Worship gives clarity to hear God's voice... (Psalm 29:2)
Worship produces righteousness... (Psalm 132:7-9)
Worship produces strength to overcome... (Psalm 138:2)
Worship forces the enemy to leave your atmosphere... (Matthew 4:10, 11)
The time to worship is NOW... (John 4:23)
God is searching for worshippers... (John 4:23)
Worship produces revelation... (Acts 8: 27- 32)
Worship kills the flesh... (Philippians 3:3)

WORSHIP CREATES A CLIMATE OF UNITY... You can't enter into God's presence if you are offended at someone. Worship creates a climate of unity. The word declares in Psalm 133, *"How good and pleasant it is for men to walk in unity for it is like the oil that flows..."* The anointing that changes things flows in the power of real worship.

WORSHIP CREATES PEACE... Will you do what it takes to become a favored worshipper? Take the time necessary to move into God's presence. Stop being influenced by things that don't really matter. You are going to have to be a worshipper if you want a life of peace. In God's presence there's peace. I know that right now you are becoming a worshipper...

Do it now! Just stop what you're doing, lift up your voice and sing to the Lord. **Worship Him!** I know you will never be the same. Remember, the proof of His presence is change.

Week Fifteen

AGREEMENT UNLOCKS THE OIL

"Behold, how good and how pleasant it is for brethren to dwell together in unity! It is like the precious ointment upon the head that ran down upon the beard even Aaron's beard: that went down to the skirts of his garments." Psalm 133:1-2

AGREEMENT RELEASES THE OIL...

We are actually walking in unity with one another when we come together in agreement.

There is power in agreement. Agreement means we are going the same way.

- *Agreement releases the oil of others to flow.*
- *Agreement releases the oil of the Holy Spirit to flow.*
- *Favor flows when the Holy Spirit is moving.*

How good and pleasant it is for men to walk in agreement. Something happens around you when someone comes into agreement with you. Their ability to recognize what's in you releases what's in you to flow.

Jesus didn't help anyone who didn't first recognize who He was. When they recognized Him, they came into agreement with Him, and something around them changed.

Many haven't experienced change because they are always in disagreement to what the Lord is doing. Today, we are going to work on walking in agreement. How can two walk together unless they're in agreement? We love to preach about submission, yet submission only begins when agreement ends.

Yes, we need to learn how to submit when we don't agree, but I don't want someone to stay around me if every time I make a decision to do something, they are always walking in submission. "I don't agree, but I'll submit…" Please! This only means that now, I'm going to have to carry you all the way.

People like this never carry their own load, and when the going gets tough, they'll be the very ones letting you know that they were never in agreement to the decision anyway. I need someone to come along side of me and say, "I'm with you. I'm in agreement. Let's carry this load together." When this happens, something is released in both of us that will cause our gifts, our anointing, and our talents to flow. The agreement releases the oil. When we come into agreement with God's Word, it causes the oil of the Word to be released.

GOD IS PRESENT IN THE ATMOSPHERE OF AGREEMENT…

When we gather together in His name in our churches, or at a home group, we cause something supernatural to take place. God is present in the group walking among us, seeking to release His Spirit on us.

"Again I say unto you, that if two of you shall agree on earth as touching any thing that they shall ask, it shall be done for them of my Father which is in heaven. For where two or three are gathered together in my name, there am I in the midst of them."
Mathew 18:19-20

AGREEMENT RELEASES THE OIL OF PEACE...

How good and pleasant it is! Agreement produces a peaceful atmosphere. Agreement in a marriage causes the two, to focus on what needs to be done, rather than what's not being done.

THE NEMESIS TO AGREEMENT IS DIVISION...

Divorce is the result of walking in disagreement. Agreement builds, but disagreements will tear down what agreement has been building. People will eventually become stressed in a relationship, whether marriage, or friendship, if they can't walk in agreement. Division will be the result of disagreement, and those two people will eventually separate. If we can't fix the problem, the relationship is over.

Division is two visions that try to exist in one house. Division produces stress... Division produces struggle... Division produces strife... Stop disagreement because it will eventually cause division.

AGREEMENT TAKES THE STRUGGLE OUT OF SUCCESS...

More can be accomplished when two come in agreement. The word of God says, "One can put a thousand to flight, but two of you can put ten thousand to flight." (Deuteronomy 32:30).

Agreement takes the struggle out of success. Find someone today that can come in agreement with you over a situation and see how much faster your answer will come.

"And five of you shall chase an hundred, and an hundred of you shall put ten thousand to flight: and your enemies shall fall before you by the sword." Leviticus 26:8 KJV

THE DAY OF PENTECOST WAS BIRTHED ON THE BACK OF AGREEMENT...

"And when the day of Pentecost was fully come, they were all with one accord in one place. And suddenly there came a sound from heaven as of a rushing mighty wind, and it filled the entire house where they were sitting." Acts 2:1-2

AGREEMENT PRODUCES THE JOY OF REAL WORSHIP...

AGREEMENT PRODUCES A GREAT MARRIAGE...

AGREEMENT BUILDS A SOLID CHURCH...

"And they, continuing daily with one accord in the temple, and breaking bread from house to house, did eat their meat with gladness and singleness of heart, Praising God, and having favor with all the people. **"And the Lord added to the church daily such as should be saved."** Acts 2:46-47

AGREEMENT RELEASES THE OIL OF HEALING TO FLOW IN YOUR LIFE...

"And by the hands of the apostles were many signs and wonders wrought among the people; (and they were all with one accord in Solomon's porch. And of the rest durst no man joins himself to them: but the people magnified them. And believers were the more added to the Lord, multitudes both of men and women.)" Acts 5:12-14

AGREEMENT WILL DRIVE OUT UNCLEAN SPIRITS...

"And the people with one accord gave heed unto those things which Philip spake, hearing and seeing the miracles, which he did. For unclean spirits, crying with loud voice came out of many that were possessed with them: and many taken with palsies, and that were lame, were healed." Acts 8:6-7

AGREEMENT PRODUCES JOY IN A CHURCH AND CITY....

"...and there was great joy in that city." Acts 8:8

AGREEMENT BRINGS JOY INTO YOUR HOME...

Again, the nemesis to agreement is a divided heart. No leader can build their organization, whether it is a business, or a church, if there are divided hearts in the crowd. Even the Lord couldn't lead those who were divided. The rich young ruler wouldn't make that choice and come into agreement to Jesus' words. Why? He had a divided heart.

"No one can serve two masters; for either he will hate the one and love the other, or else he will be loyal to the one and despise the other. You cannot serve God and mammon." Matthew 6:24 NKJV

I read a book that was awesome on the favor of agreement by Dr. Thomas Michael, "The Agreement, Unlocking the Favor of God." Let me quote a part of what Dr. Michael says. "The purpose of agreement is unity... the fruit of agreement is favor... the fragrance of agreement is worship..." I think this book is one of the best manuscripts I've read on the power of agreement.

COME OUT OF AGREEMENT WITH FALSE IDOLS...

"And what agreement hath the temple of God with idols? For ye are the temple of the living God; as God hath said, I will dwell in

them, and walk in them; and I will be their God, and they shall be my people. Wherefore come out from among them, and be ye separate, saith the Lord, and touch not the unclean thing; and I will receive you." 2 Corinthians 6:16-17

Hell has attacked our churches, our homes and our businesses with the spirit of division. We can't build when we are using all of our efforts trying to keep the peace in our lives. How can your pastor build the church according to what the Lord has called him to do, if he constantly has to explain himself to those who are never in agreement? He can't! Stop making excuses and blaming those who could be doing great things for you and take a look; the reason you are not being successful could be that you have fallen out of agreement with their vision. Now, both of you are struggling to succeed. The focus isn't on the oil; it's on the power of unity. Offer up a prayer today. Ask the Lord to put you in agreement with those He has placed over you. Read the word of God and come in agreement with it. You will release its oil to flow over your life. There's healing in that agreement… there's peace in that agreement… there's restoration in that agreement.

Week Sixteen

CASUAL CHRISTIANITY PRODUCES CASUALITIES

What does it mean to be a casual Christian? Are you a casual Christian? You might be and not even know it. There are scriptures in the book of Revelation that puts this question in my heart. Jesus speaks to John about the seven churches, and He begins to describe the Church of the Laodiceans. Jesus says, *"I know your works, you are neither cold nor hot; but because you are lukewarm (casual) I will spit you out of my mouth"* (Revelation 3:14-16). Jesus would rather you be cold, or hot; not somewhere in the middle. It is better to be cold and never be around the fire... better to be those who aren't even in church... those who don't pay tithes... those living a life of sin, than to be a casual Christian.

Webster's dictionary defines *casual* as, "Happening by chance; **not planned**; incidental [a *casual* visit]; happening, active, etc. at **irregular intervals**; **occasional** [a *casual* worker]...**slight**

or superficial [a *casual* acquaintance] *a*) **careless or cursory** [far too *casual* in his methods] *b*) **nonchalant; dispassionate** [affecting *casual* unconcern] *a*) **informal or relaxed** [a *casual* atmosphere] *b*) **designed for informal occasions** or use [*casual* clothes]" ©1995 Zane Publishing, Inc. ©1994, 1991, 1988 Simon & Schuster, Inc.

I've met many casual Christians in my twenty-five years of ministry. I had them help me start my church. They wanted God to move and do certain things, as long as He didn't mess with their lives, or busy schedules. They would come to church occasionally... they would tithe occasionally... they would do certain things occasionally... but they were never consistent.

Usually the wealthy people in a congregation are those who can afford to go away on the weekends. They are the ones who attend church for a few weeks, and then you don't see them.

Are you reading this and feeling a tug? Could you possibly be lukewarm, casual? Don't panic or get mad. There's hope! You can confess your weaknesses, repent, and God will begin to build a fire under you. You see, lukewarm is dangerous because it's a place of comfort. It's religion at its best. At least being cold will cause you to search for the fire, to release the pain of freezing. But casual! My heart breaks for those who can't even see that they are casual. When they get to heaven they will find out they were living a lie the whole time. Let's look at more verses in Revelation; notice the attitude of this church.

"Because thou sayest, I am rich, and increased with goods, and have need of nothing; and knowest not that thou art wretched, and miserable, and poor, and blind, and naked." Revelation 3:17

Prosperity can be more dangerous than poverty. When you're wealthy, the tendency is to become self-sufficient. God is okay as long as He stays away from their comfort. God forbid a man of God challenge these kinds of people and put them in check about their **casual lifestyle.** What they need to understand is, when much is given, much will be required.

CASUAL WALK...

Let me caution you, complacency is a sin. Casual worship and causal lifestyles cause complacency. **The secret of your success is hidden in your daily routine. Successful people do daily what unsuccessful people do occasionally.**

What you do daily is deciding what you are becoming.

How can we expect God to bless us with His fullness if we live for Him casually? A nonchalant, occasional, and mediocre walk will produce a casual witness.

CASUAL WITNESS...

What should be the goal of all Christians? **To be a witness!**

*"But ye shall receive power, after that the Holy Ghost is come upon you: and ye **shall be witnesses** unto me both in Jerusalem, and in all Judaea, and in Samaria, and unto the uttermost part of the earth."* Acts 1:8

The Greek translation of *'witnesses'* is *'martyr'*. You will be a willing victim for the cause of truth. Do you think you can be a witness, a willing victim, living a casual walk? The purpose of salvation is to be a powerful witness for Christ. I am horrified when I see the witness of people who claim to be Christians. It's too easy to become casual.

What was the great commission? *"Go and make disciples..."* Let's not make casual disciples. We need to check ourselves before we wreck ourselves. How can we be a great witness if we can't be consistent, passionate and purposeful about what we believe?

*"Having therefore obtained help of God, I continue unto this day, **witnessing** both to small and great, saying none other things than those which the prophets and Moses did say should come."* Acts 26:22

CASUAL WARFARE...

If we are casual in our walk and casual in our witness, then we will become casual in our warfare. How can any person believe that they can win a war if they are not committed to die for what they believe? Right now, while I'm writing, there are American soldiers overseas fighting a tyranny of ignorance; risking their lives for what we believe in, democracy. Are these men and women walking around in a strange country with a casual attitude? "Maybe I'm a soldier today, maybe not." No, they are soldiers everyday. If they become nonchalant and casual, it may cost them their life and the lives of others. Don't become so enamored with grace that you forget we are at war! This warfare is not fleshly, but spiritual, and this warfare we are fighting is going to be won. We've actually already won; we are just waiting for the manifestation of our complete victory. (2 Corinthians 10: 4)

Stop using excuses and making grace a license to do what is casual. God is not going to bless those who are living a casual Christian life. Lukewarm isn't going to cut it in the end.

Today, make your prayer, a prayer to stop being UNINVOLVED with godly things. Ask your church leaders what you can do to get involved with advancing God's house. Don't just put your money in! Put yourself in! The focus you place on God's affairs will determine the focus God puts on your affairs.

Week Seventeen

IGNORING THE FIRE BY LOOKING TOO LONG AT THE FURNACE

DON'T BE SO FOCUSED ON THE FURNACE THAT YOU FORGET THE FIRE...

"... Always learning and never able to come to the knowledge of the truth..." 2 Timothy 3:6-8 NKJV

There are those who only worship the furnace, forgetting the whole purpose of the furnace is to house the fire.

Process is necessary, and I believe in the process of time and the scheduling of seasons. Satan's greatest weapon is to rob us of timing and seasons. Religion is when we forget about the fire and only worry about the process; the outward appearances, the buildings instead of His presence... the outcome instead of His purpose... the applause of men instead of the applause of heaven... entertainment instead of ministering... what others think instead of what God thinks... ego builders instead of faith builders.

RELIGION IS MAN'S ATTEMPT TO PLEASE GOD MAN'S WAY...

Religion is the attempt to make a spiritual place where man's spiritual duties can be satisfied; a place where people are made to feel good about themselves without any conviction to change, or to become a better spiritual being. Churches have become a place where we sing and listen to sermons, but never unlock the gifts of the Spirit. When we feel we've done our part, we leave and never consider asking the question, "Was God pleased with my worship today?"

RELIGION IS MAN'S ATTEMPT TO EXPLAIN GOD AND GODLY THINGS MAN'S WAY...

I've met people who attend dead churches but are so alive and willing to grow to a deeper walk in the Spirit; however, they can't break the connection of their religion. They will make comments like, "There's got to be more to the Lord than this?" **THERE IS!** "I wish we would worship God longer." **YOU SHOULD!** "Why can't we see healings and the gifts move more in our church?" **YOU CAN!**

Stop staying connected to the process of a dead house. What good is the furnace if the fire is gone out?

THE PASSION TO HURT OTHERS REVEALS THE NATURE OF A PERSON...

I am amazed at the depravity of the human race. I am shocked when I see how easy it is for men to abuse and hurt others.

The world is walking in distrust and paranoia. No wonder, when what we see in the news is the horror of what people say about each other and the hate that exists around us. When the world happens to visit our local churches, sad to say, they are not greeted with the power of the gospel of Jesus Christ, not with the hand of healing, or the heart of restoration; instead they are greeted with the smile of religion! The passion of the gospel however, is to remove pain, not inflict it.

- Jesus is life, not death…
- Jesus is love, not hate…
- Jesus is healing, not pain…

Facts about religion…………
Religion produces loss better than it produces increase…
Religion manipulates better than it motivates…
Religion defeats better than it delivers…
Religion destroys better than it develops…
Religion tears down better than it builds up…
Religion hurts better than it heals…
Religion judges better than it forgives…
Religion controls better than it conforms…
Religion crucifies better than it changes…
Religion stagnates better than it elevates…
Religion isolates better than it congregates…
Religion hates better than it loves…

Run from any organization that becomes religious in its structure and doesn't allow room for the organization to change and grow. Run when those around you are controlling those appointed over you.

*Law of the lid…*Dr. John Maxwell wrote a book entitled "21 Irrefutable Laws of Leadership." There is a chapter in this book on the "Law of the Lid". How can you grow in your church if the man over you is at a spiritual five on the scale of one to ten and you desire to be an eight? **You can't!** What if a pastor wants to move in the gifts, but has a congregation so steeped in traditions that they won't let him? He wants to be a ten, but his congregation, who can fire him, is satisfied with being a six. The lid that sits over you sets the limit on how you can grow. This is why I have such a problem with Pentecostal Christians leaving Pentecostal churches to go to nominal churches that don't believe in the Pentecostal doctrine. Many are leaving out of hurt, but realize they desire more than what they are receiving after they've left. They'll start having a Bible study at their house and try to get others to operate in the gifts that the headship strongly disagrees with. This so called "spirit-filled" group is now operating in a demonic spirit. "How can you say that?" you may ask. Any group is out of spiritual order if the head of that church doesn't sanction what they're doing. You can't raise the leaders' lid for them; they must be willing to raise it for themselves.

KNOWLEDGE WITHOUT SPIRIT IS USELESS...

Paul told Timothy that in the last days there would be stressful times. Church people would be in love with what pleases them instead of what changes them. That we would see a great waxing cold of the fire and there would be a spirit of anger and rebellion like none we have ever seen. Children would become disobedient to their parents.

"For men shall be lovers of their own selves, covetous, boasters, proud, blasphemers, disobedient to parents, unthankful, unholy, Without natural affection, trucebreakers, false accusers, incontinent, fierce, despisers of those that are good, Traitors, heady, high-minded, lovers of pleasures more than lovers of God."
2 Timothy 3:2-4

In verse five, Paul says that people would have a form of godliness, but deny the power. Have a form; they were caught up in the form, or the structure; the furnace without the fire. When there is only a form, all you have is the structure of something without the life of the Spirit, and there will be no heat, no joy and no change...just going through the motions. God help me! I will not attend a church that isn't moving in the gifts. I need more than just four songs, a sermon, and home by high noon. I need a messenger who has heard from God to bring me a message that will speak into my life and ignite my faith.

WHERE THERE IS NO WOOD THE FIRE WILL GO OUT... You will not be able to supply the wood that will keep the fire lit in your church if you do not want to move into greater gifts. Your willingness to be changed gives the fire of the Holy Spirit the wood necessary to keep the fire burning bright. Most people in our churches want the knowledge of God, but avoid the truth. These kinds of people are always learning, or being taught, but never coming to the knowledge of truth. *"Ever learning and never able to come to the knowledge of the truth..."* 2 Timothy 3:7

FIRE EXPOSES WHAT DOESN'T BELONG... Not everybody around you belongs around you. Satan's main reason for keeping us away from the fire is because he knows that the fire will expose what doesn't belong. Move closer to the fire of the Spirit if you want to reveal those around you who don't belong.

"And when Paul had gathered a bundle of sticks, and laid them on the fire, there came a viper out of the heat, and fastened on his hand." Acts 28:3

Disguised as a stick in the arms of Paul was a viper; if Paul had stayed away from the fire, he would have never noticed that he was carrying danger. The heat of the fire forced the viper to reveal itself. Can you imagine how many vipers are hanging around a dead church? Years ago, I preached at a church, and I was horrified at how the people in this church were fighting the very truth of God's word. They had such a spirit of control. The leaders in this church were so bad they wouldn't even call their Senior Pastor by his title, and they got indignant when I asked them to. There was no Spirit in this church at all. Their worship was cold... their giving was cold... their love was cold. I don't just blame them; I also blame this Pastor who wouldn't stand up and make changes...fearful of losing tithe payers. *You cannot change what you tolerate.*

These people had the form of church, but no fire. This Pastor cried to me, telling me that no one had ever given him anything in the church, and He had been there for over ten years. He expressed to me how he hated being there and how he wished God would move him. God will never promote you until you become over-qualified in your present position. I told him that he should do something about it. He said, "Well, they're good people." My reply was, "good ungodly people..." "Anyone who fights the truth of change is ungodly." The road to hell is paved with good people with good intentions.

"ADVERSARIES DECIDE REWARDS" Mike Murdock

When you do what others are unwilling to do you will receive the spoils of your warfare. If you will fight this warfare of religion, and begin to add wood to the fire, you will begin to experience God's prosperity.

Let's ask the Lord to open our eyes. Let's not stay stuck in religion, and in the process miss the greatest part of being saved. We are not saved just to make heaven and miss hell. We are saved to walk in the Spirit of all of God's blessings.

Today is your day for a miracle. Seek the gifts with love. Ask the Holy Spirit to fill you today with His understanding. You matter to Him. He wants to teach you the ways of the Lord. He wants to give you the fire...

Week Eighteen

BETTER TO BE KNOWN THAN JUST KNOW

I've placed this topic next because it goes along with what we've learned about religion in the last chapter.

One of the greatest scriptures to me is the one where Jesus compares the Kingdom of Heaven to those who say, "Lord, Lord, didn't we cast out demons in your name, and do signs and wonders..."

*"Not every one that saith unto me, Lord, Lord, shall enter into the kingdom of heaven; but he that doeth the will of my Father which is in heaven. Many will say to me in that day, Lord, Lord, have we not prophesied in thy name? and in thy name have cast out devils? and in thy name done many wonderful works? And then will I profess unto them, **I never knew you**: depart from me, ye that work iniquity."* Matthew 7:21-23

What grabs my attention at first glance is that these people had the form of something that could have been mistaken as God's approval. It's obvious that they were called to do the work. What happened? Surely when they started they had the right motive. I can't believe that people would enter the ministry for any other reason than to please the Lord.

Somewhere on their journey they got caught up in the form of godliness and lost the spirit of what they were doing. They were anointed to function successfully in their ministry, but not in their walk.

BEING ANOINTED DOESN'T MEAN YOU'RE WALKING ACCORDING TO GOD'S WORD...

If we've learned anything about history, we should have learned that there were men in times past that operated in great miraculous powers, and performed signs and wonders that would astound the most skeptical. These ministers performed great things, yet, they were men who had strong vices that controlled them.

I have heard stories about men who would lay down their liquor bottle, walk out on the platform and were still anointed to do the work. Blind eyes would be healed... the deaf would hear... cancers would fall off... great miracles would take place, yet, their lifestyles were in question. You may be thinking, how is this going to help me? Stay with me through the whole chapter, and you'll see the power of being known, verses knowing. You must realize that your walk must be just as important as your work. We should not be so focused on our work that we forget how to walk with the Lord.

It's obvious that you can have an anointed ministry and lose your personal walk. There is no special power to righteousness no matter how anointed someone is. We all have to walk the same. We must all pray... we must all study God's word... we must all walk in love. Concentrate more on pleasing the Lord rather than growing a great ministry.

SUCCESS DOESN'T MEAN GOD IS IN APPROVAL OF YOUR LIFESTYLE...

Don't mistake prosperity and increase as God's approval of your lifestyle. What you're doing isn't as important as what you're becoming. Character is more important than performance.

Don't let the blessings of God take you where character can't keep you. Character is what you are, not what you are doing. God isn't going to judge us just for what we've done. We are also responsible to take the time necessary to get in God's presence.

The verse today clearly states that there were those who performed for God and were successful in their ministry. They knew God, but *knowing* wasn't as important, as being *known*. "Lord, Lord, didn't we...?" Notice His response; "Depart from me for I never *knew* you." Does the Lord *know* you today? Think for a moment, many of us have heard of Bishop T.D. Jakes. If I asked you if you know him, you would probably answer yes. But, does Bishop Jakes know you? More than likely, not! The ability to know someone is easy when they are visible on television. There must be time spent together to know, or have a relationship with someone.

"And Enoch walked with God; and he was not, for God took him." Genesis 5:24. NKJV

Enoch walked with God until he was not... You may enter into a relationship with the Lord carrying your shortcomings. You may enter addicted to drugs... you may enter with a bitterness problem... you may enter this walk with marital issues... The key is to enter, through the blood and sacrifice of Jesus.

Enoch created an atmosphere that was inviting to God's presence. God came down and spent days with Enoch until one day, God took Enoch with Him. The more Enoch walked with God, the more God got to know Enoch; the more we walk with the Lord, the more like the Lord we become. When He appears we will be like Him...

*"Beloved, now are we the sons of God, and it doth not yet appear what we shall be: but we know that, when he shall appear, **we shall be like him**; for we shall see him as he is."* 1 John 3:2

I want to be *known* by the Lord as much as I want to know Him. It's my desire to take the time necessary to become *known* by the Lord; doing what is required of my life's example, getting the job done and being found worthy of His love, not just being talented and able to perform. I want to be more interested in living the message than preaching the message. Take the time today to live the message; to become *known* and not just to know. Knowledge void of Jesus is dangerous and useless.

Week Nineteen

THE BURDEN OF FAVOR!

You're going to have to be trusted to carry God's burden if you are going to walk in the blessings of the Lord. Now, don't panic, the Lord Himself told us that His burden is light; however, there is still a price to be favored.

Before you can experience the favor of God, you must understand that blessings come with burden. The dictionary says that a *burden* is *a load, duty, responsibility, to be weighed down.*

You can't carry the harvest of favor, if you can't carry the burden. People are driven to look at success and successful people wishing they could have what they have yet, they never stop to consider what they did to produce what they have. God starts us small and works us to His abundance. Man, on the other hand, wants to start off big and usually ends up small. Remember, the "end of a thing is better." Be patient, your harvest has already been sent!

GOD DESIRES TO RELEASE HIS FAVOR... It is God's desire to bless you. God isn't holding back your financial blessing; He doesn't desire for any of us to be sick.

"Let them shout for joy, and be glad, that favour my righteous cause: yea, let them say continually, Let the LORD be magnified, which hath pleasure in the prosperity of his servant." Psalm 35:27

RESPONSBILITY PRODUCES FAVOR... *"For every man shall bear his own burden."* Galatians 6:5

Blessings are scheduled at the end of your burden. Rewards are the result of completing an assignment. Have you ever noticed ministers who wear ministerial uniforms with white collars? Most of us have no idea why they are wearing those uniforms. You probably thought they were just wearing them because they were trying to stand out in a crowd. Not so. The white collar means that they have taken a vow to be yoked to the ministry. They have decided to carry the weight of their ministry and to help those they are assigned to.

I want the favor of God to fall on your life and on your whole family.

Most men of God are incapable of carrying the full load and burden of their present ministry, much less take care of their personal life, such as their spouse and children. They are in need of someone they can trust to help them carry the burden of their ministry.

THE BURDEN OF FAVOR IS LOYALTY... Loyalty is staying true to a person when circumstances have changed. Loyalty is defined as an obligation to defend, support, or to be true to. Faithful!

LOYALTY IS A SEED INTO ANOTHER MAN'S HARVEST... When you're loyal to a person you are serving, you open yourself up to receive blessings from them. Loyalty is a seed into another person's promotion, and carrying the burden of favor can produce uncommon favor from the person you are being loyal to. You may not have money seeds to sow; can you sow your

commitment of loyalty?

ONE OF GOD'S GREATEST GIFTS TO YOU IS LOYALTY... It takes loyalty from someone for a person to accomplish what God has assigned them to accomplish. Jonathan informed his armor bearer of his intentions to cross the ravine and encounter the enemy. Jonathan's armor bearer is not just the servant in this story; he's the key to success. His loyalty enabled him to find a season of favor and enabled his leader to conquer. His answer was, *"Do all that you have in mind," his armor-bearer said. "Go ahead; I am with you heart and soul."* 1 Samuel 14:7 NIV

I love that answer! **Do all that you have in your heart (mind); I am with you heart and soul.** He was declaring that he was willing to carry this burden and follow him. The armor bearer, or his assistant, was helping Jonathan conquer the problem. His willingness to bear the burden of battle without knowing the outcome, facing the enemy, climbing the ravine, and standing behind his leader, actually lead him straight into his season of favor. The armor bearer could have been killed with his leader that day. I believe that the relationship between Jonathan and his armor bearer was never the same after that day.

SECOND BUT SATISFIED... I understand the grace and power of serving. I served senior pastors for fifteen years while youth pastoring, and the one thing I can say about myself was that I was a good servant. I never even felt like I was in a lesser position when I carried their brief cases, picked up their stuff, made sure they looked good and served the man of God in any way possible to make his life easier. I was loyal. I knew that what I was doing was important! Actually, I wasn't serving a man; I was serving God in the man. Yes, when he was awake I was awake. When he was working, I was working. When he was mad, I was the go between; allowing my senior pastor to unload on me so he would not expose himself to his people. Sometimes the burden was hard, but I served with loyalty.

Now, I'm the leader, I'm the Bishop, I'm the author, and there are men assigned to me. The seed of loyalty I planted has produced a harvest of loyalty in my life.

Praise the Lord for being allowed the position to serve. If you're not serving, carrying the weight of a church, or a man of God; ask the Lord to allow you the privilege of becoming what I believe, is the greatest position in the Kingdom. Second and satisfied! You will graduate and be promoted when you've passed the test of loyalty. Learn to be a great burden bearer so that God will promote you to be a great leader.

Lord, I speak over my precious reader today. I ask You to send a season of favor and peace. Help them to see themselves as great in any position. Lift their hearts to Your presence and drive away anything that is attacking them. In Jesus name AMEN!

Week Twenty

MOUTH- TO- MOUTH RESTORATION

MOUTH TO EAR DEVASTATION

"They overcame him by the blood of the Lamb and by the word of their testimony; they did not love their lives so much as to shrink from death." Revelation 12:11 NIV

"The woman was given the two wings of a great eagle, so that she might fly to the place prepared for her in the desert, where she would be taken care of for a time, times and half a time, out of the serpent's reach. Then from his mouth the serpent spewed water like a river, to overtake the woman and sweep her away with the torrent. But the earth helped the woman by opening its mouth and swallowing the river that the dragon had spewed out of his mouth." Revelation 12:14-16 NIV

Revelation 12:11 is one of the most quoted verses about being an over-comer, but I believe we usually leave out what is the most powerful key to the verse when we quote it. *"They overcame him by the blood of the lamb and by the word of their testimony and they did not shrink back..."*

WORDS ARE THE NEUTRALIZING POWER TO THE SERPENT'S ACID...

The dragon, which is Satan, is not going to reveal himself when he comes. The dragon's greatest weapon is darkness. He's like a stealth bomber; you won't know he's there until you hear the power of his lies slamming on the soil of your life. Satan will begin to gain access to your ear if you don't learn how to expose him in the power of God's truth (Word of God spoken). When you start listening, you have already lost the fight. He's too powerful and masterful with words to try and play mental games with. You and I must stop his voice the very minute he speaks. Trust me; Satan's been watching mankind for seven thousand years. You think he might understand us better than we understand him?

The book of Revelation reveals that water comes out of the dragon's mouth when he opens it. Water represents spirit. Wait a minute, I thought dragons spit out fire, not water? This dragon has learned the lingo of religion. He's coming in as an angel of light.

"And no wonder, for Satan himself masquerades as an angel of light. It is not surprising, then, if his servants masquerade as servants of righteousness. Their end will be what their actions deserve." 2 Corinthians 11:14-15 NIV

We read in Revelation chapter 12:16 that the earth helped the women. How did the earth do that? She opened up her mouth and swallowed up the water. I believe that the earth represents the saints who have overcome, and they are now using the power of God's Word to counter attack the poison of the dragon. When

Satan speaks, speak back!

STOP SAYING WHAT YOU SEE AND START SEEING WHAT YOU SAY...

Most people only see what's going on around them. What you're facing doesn't necessarily mean it is truth. There is our truth, and then, there is God's truth. Don't listen when the dragon speaks; speak back, immediately! Give him the power of God's Word. Speak the real truth, not the truth you see, but the truth that faith is seeing. When the dragon says cancer, you neutralize that acid with, "NO, I'm healed by the blood!" When he says poverty, you say, "Prosperity!" When he says sick, you say, "Healed!" When he says divorce, you say "Restoration"... See how this formula works? Buy one of those promise books that are sold in the local bookstore. Let me recommend a good book for you by Dr. Mike Murdock, "58 Blessings..." You can order it on his website www.mikemurdock.com.

Today, we are more than conquers! Speak the word! Mouth to mouth restoration vs. mouth to ear devastation.

Let me give you a closing thought for today from Isaiah.

*"When the enemy comes in like a flood, the Spirit of the LORD will lift up a **standard** against him. "As for Me," says the LORD, "this is My covenant with them: My Spirit who is upon you, and **My words** which I have put in your **mouth**, shall not depart from **your mouth**, nor from the **mouth** of your descendants, nor from the **mouth** of your descendants' descendants," says the LORD, "from this time and forevermore."* Isaiah 59:19, 21 NKJV

Week Twenty - One

FACE IT! FIX IT! FORGET IT!

*"**B**rethren, I count not myself to have apprehended: but this one thing I do, forgetting those things, which are behind, and reaching forth unto those things, which are before, I press toward the mark for the prize of the high calling of God in Christ Jesus. Let us therefore, as many as be perfect, be thus minded: and if in any thing ye be otherwise minded, God shall reveal even this unto you."* Philippians 3:13-15

A good friend of mine, Dr. Michael Chitwood, was speaking at the 2004, "Uncommon Millionaire Conference" in Dallas, Texas. He made a statement to the people, "Face it, fix it, forget it!"

Paul was speaking in the terms of their financial crisis and mistakes. I couldn't help but pick up this simple, but true principle on how we should live and respond to all of life's problems. One of the hardest things to do in life is to live without having to be reminded of what we did in our past. The enemy loves to point out

TODAY'S MESS IS TOMORROW'S MESSAGE!

all of our mistakes and has no problem reminding us what a real failure we are on a daily basis. When the enemy isn't reminding us of our past, our friends are, and if our friends aren't reminding us, then we have to fight our mind that seems to never be remised of what we have done in our past.

Life seems to have this uncanny power to schedule pain, problems and circumstances without even consoling us. *Bad things are happening everyday to good people.* We must understand that what we've experienced in the past is nothing more than our testimony in our present and the springboard to our future. Problems are not prejudice; they will enter anyone's life at anytime, and your economic status, or racial color has no power to keep it at bay.

The longer I live the more I understand that my life is nothing more than a living message of what I have survived. Face it, who wants someone to help them who hasn't been through and survived their own troubles and hurts? Not me!

YOU WILL NEVER MOVE FORWARD UNTIL YOU HAVE RELEASED WHERE YOU CAME FROM.

My family and I visited New York City for Christmas one year. The day we were returning home, we rode a shuttle bus to LaGuardia Airport. I realized, as we rode through the city, that we were taking the same route that my family and I had walked everyday. I was sitting there, looking at all the places that we had been and realized something. I was in my present looking at my past. No one can escape having a past. You started this book in your present that has now become your past.

YOU MUST FACE YOUR PAST... FORGIVE YOUR WRONG DOINGS AND THEN MOVE ON.

Your past gives your present life meaning and hope for your future. The truth is that people will only succeed when they face their past, deal with their hurt and wrong decisions, and fix it. How do you fix it? Forgiving what's hurt you in your past gives you the power to exit your past and start entering your future.

Your mess is nothing more than the beginning of your message. How do you spell message? MESS-AGE! Add age to a mess and you have a message.

Time is the important ingredient to a mess. The more you can survive the pain, the longer you can stay alive; you will eventually grow through your mess and turn it into your message. Your history will become someone's answer for the reason they can survive their hurts.

LEARN FROM YOUR PAST, DON'T LIVE IN IT...

There is so much we can gain from where we came from. The only reason most haven't is because they allow the wrong doings of their past to control and manipulate them from learning and moving beyond it. The pain of remembering causes people to hide, and hiding causes them not to experience and live in their present. The hurts in their past, such as wrong financial decisions, being betrayed by someone they assumed was close to them, parental abuse, or child molestation, an over possessive father, an under affectionate mother; there is always, something living in the closet of the past. The tendency of most is to shut those hurts and pains in that closet, lock the door and throw away the key hoping never to have to deal with them again.

What if you open that door right now and let the healing, loving power of God have those mistakes and messes? What can it hurt? Think about it, have you been running all of this time from what is in that closet? If you're like me, every time you even start getting close to God, that door always starts trying to become the focus. That mess can become your message! You have aged since then. That's not you anymore. You are not the same person you were when you made those mistakes. Your mess is the power to your message. Your past is adding meaning to your life. Go ahead, open that door today, and let the power of God heal what's been hurting you.

STOP LIVING IN THE PAST.

There are those who never leave the hurts of their past. They just live in that pain until there is no happiness and no hope. They begin to live in fear of repeating the past. They are stuck in the past, having to be dulled day after day with the reminder that if they start living they may have to face and release the past. People who live in their past never experience the power of freedom in their present. They are constantly walking in fear, waiting for someone to do to them in their present, what their father, mother, boyfriend, or girlfriend did in their past. Stop the insanity! Stop what you're doing and just open the door to all of your hurts and mistakes. Forgive yourself and those who may have hurt you.

Face it, **Fix it** and you guessed it, **time to move on**! To move on, you're going to have to **forget it**. How can you forget?

STEPS TO TOTAL FREEDOM FROM YOUR MISTAKES; TURNING YOUR MESS INTO YOUR MESSAGE

- Face your mistakes…
- Forgive yourself for making the mistake...
- Forgive those you are angry with…
- Fix your mistake by repenting to God and making the necessary changes to total recovery…
- Release the curse and bondage of guilt that is holding you in captivity…
- Forget it by releasing your mind from thinking about it…
- Go ahead and tell your heart to be healed. Give yourself permission to be OKAY!

Week Twenty - Two

NO PRICE – NO PASSION

"No one will ever understand your praise until they have understood your pain" Bishop T.D. Jakes

Those who haven't paid your price will never understand your passion. Success in any form, whether it is relational, or business, has a price.

Success has a price tag and it's not on sale. You're not going to find what you need to succeed on the clearance rack of life. You're not going to find it at a discount store. If you want to succeed in life, know this one truth, there is a price tag to every season of increase. Those who can pay the price have the merchandise. Those who can't, will either hate you for it, or try to steal it from you.

STOP TRYING TO PLEASE EVERYONE.

Allow me to let you in on a little secret. You can't, and won't, please everyone.

It's impossible to live a life of growth and success trying to make everyone around you comfortable. This will absolutely not happen. The quicker you accept this, the faster you can move on to purchase your success. I'm not implicating that success can be purchased with money. No, the currency you're going to need is the understanding that people will either add to you, or take away from you. Those who haven't paid your price won't understand your passion.

NOT EVERYONE AROUND YOU IS GOOD FOR YOU.

Don't be alarmed when you see people leaving your life. Let them go! I started my church with a small group of people. I had so many who treated me with love and accepted me with all my mistakes. Things changed when I began to increase and grow, and started realizing my position as the "set man," or the chief leader over my church and began to take my place as the builder of my church. Those who said they would never leave; did! I went on an inward journey of depression and hurt for the longest time after that; wondering what was wrong with me. God placed a man in my life, a mentor, Dr. Mike Murdock, and he said something to me that has not stopped ringing in my spirit.

THOSE WHO ARE EXITING YOUR LIFE MAY HAVE BEEN DISQUALIFIED FOR YOUR HARVEST.

When you see an exodus taking place around you, it's because those who are leaving didn't qualify for your harvest. Stop hurting over those who are leaving. God's trying to get your harvest to you. Stop crying about those who left, and start looking for the ones God is about to send to you.

Most people never really understand someone who has a passion for things they have built for themselves. Children that inherit money usually abuse money because they lack understanding of the sacrifice it took to make it. Most will never treat your things like you treat them because they didn't have to make a sacrifice for them and that's why I rarely loan out my things.

THOSE WHO FAIL TO RECOGNIZE YOUR VALUE AND WORTH IN LIFE DISQUALIFY FOR YOUR RELATIONSHIP.

Dr. Murdock told me something one day. I was having so much trouble with people, and it was aggravating me to the point I couldn't function correctly in my daily life. Dr. Murdock said, "Those who fail to recognize your worth disqualify for your relationship; let them go!"

That's what I did, and I've been much better for it! That's what you're going to do today. You are going to stop letting people hurt you. Remember, those who haven't paid your price will never understand your passion.

Some friendships don't last forever; they are assigned for a season. Stop trying to keep a friend that has no passion to go where you want to go and do what you want to do. Those who call themselves your friend are not always being a friend to you. The proof of friendship is loyalty. Watch those people who call you a friend, but are comfortable in your enemy's presence. I have a problem with those who feel comfortable sitting at the table with my enemy.

I know I wouldn't sit at the table if someone revealed to me they were my friend's enemy. Real friends stick up for each other! You have a question arising in your mind, *"Who is my enemy?"* How do I know them? Your enemy will materialize immediately when you announce your plans and vision.

Look around at who's becoming jealous and angry when

you begin to talk about advancement and promotion. A real friend will rejoice at the promotion of their friend. One of my good friends is, Dr. Todd Coontz, founder of Rockwealth Ministries. My heart rejoices with him when he shares his success and testimonies of what the Lord is doing in his life. We can sit for hours and talk about our advancement. Do you want to know why? Because he is my friend... we are concerned about each other's advancement.

You can't please everybody, so stop trying to. The only person I need to please in my life is God. He's the only one who is easy to please. God is the only one who knows exactly what your gifts and talents are. He understands you because He created you. God will never ask from you what you are unable to give. He will never place a demand on you that He hasn't already given you the gift, or talent to fulfill.

God is the only person around you that can truly bring peace and joy to your life. Let God in and build proper walls around you to protect your atmosphere. Never let anyone in who doesn't promote you and love the God you serve.

Week Twenty -Three

ELIGIBLE BUT NOT QUALIFIED

"F or I know the thoughts that I think toward you, saith the LORD, thoughts of peace, and not of evil, to give you an expected end." Jeremiah 29:11

If you've been saved for any length of time, you have more than likely heard this verse quoted a dozen times. Every Christian I know who has gone through, or is going through, has quoted this verse to me. *"For I know the plans I have for you, declares the LORD, plans to prosper you and not to harm you, plans to give you hope and a future."* Jeremiah 29:11 "God has a plan for me." Yes, He does!

I prefer the King James Version usage of the word **"thought,"** which is "plan" rather than the translated word that appears in the New International Version and other translations. God is letting us know that no matter how rough it gets, He's still thinking about us. This is important in understanding how the plan of God works.

GOD MOVES AT THE SPEED OF THOUGHT... We, on the other hand, move at the speed of words... Our communication is limited because we live in a three dimensional world.

This is not so with God! God doesn't move at the speed of words. He moves and operates in our lives at the speed of thought. *Imagine how unbelievable it would be if you could communicate at the speed of thought.* You could just look across the room, and whoever you're trying to communicate with would already know what to do before you say a word. Heaven operates at that kind of efficiency.

The Holy Spirit moves in the area where God is thinking, and God will only speak when the Holy Spirit is in position. This is major for us; understanding when God speaks to us and gives us an instruction, *He has already been setting up our victory. Heaven is already in position. The plan has already been worked out.*

DON'T ASSUME WHEN GOD IS SILENT THAT HE'S NOT MOVING.

DO YOU QUALIFY?

Contrary to what you may think, not everyone qualifies for Jeremiah 29:11. Now, don't get angry with me until you have finished this chapter in its entirety.

Let's look at what qualifies us to claim Jeremiah 29:11 for ourselves.

*"Now these are the words of the letter that Jeremiah the prophet sent from Jerusalem **to the remainder** of the elders who were carried away captive-to the priests, the prophets, and all the people whom Nebuchadnezzar had carried away captive from Jerusalem to Babylon."* Jeremiah 29:1-2 NKJV

Jeremiah 29:11 is written, by evidence of verse one, to the remainders; those, who are still with God even after they have gone through the warfare and captivity. They are called by God, the **"REMAINDERS."** They are the ones who haven't let the power of a crisis get the best of them. They are the elders, the priests, the prophets and all the people who are in captivity that will have to survive.

It's obvious by the next verses in this passage that this crisis isn't going to go away soon. As a matter of fact, God let's them know to go ahead, buy some land, build a house, and plant crops; this crisis has come to stay for a while. Imagine what you would feel like if you were to receive that kind of prophecy from someone. I know this, they had better know God.

I looked up the word *"remainder"* because I wanted to make sure that I qualified for Jeremiah 29:11. I was amazed at the power of this definition. This will be, by far, the deepest word you will ever see, or hear. Get ready for this meaning; it's going to unlock the power of heaven for you.

The meaning of the word *"remainder"* is, *"one who has remained."* That's what it said, but I kept on reading and here is the rest of the definition… *"What is left when a part is taken way – the rest…"* Jeremiah 29:11 was written to those who would **remain** after the clouds of pain, hurt and failure lifted.

These were the ones that God was talking to. God wanted to comfort them and inform them that no matter how hard it would be, He had a plan!

GOD HAS A PLAN!

We are going to have to survive the crisis in order to qualify for Jeremiah 29:11.

We have to understand that even Jesus had to survive His crisis to redeem us from ours. It angers me when I hear someone say you should always feel good and be happy when I know that's impossible. There is no way I'm going to always feel good and be happy. There are times when I don't feel like doing anything for God. I don't know about you, but I'm not always in the mood to shout, dance, read my Bible, or pray; but I do!

I will praise, not because I always feel like praising God, but because God deserves my praise. I understand that the more I can remain in my praise, the quicker I will get out.

I have more to write concerning Jeremiah 29:11, but for today, all I want you to do is build the power to remain through what you have already learned. Don't allow the captivity, or crisis to sidetrack you, or cause you to give up what you have already gained through your faith. Build your faith so you will not compromise and weaken your posture, or position when you find yourself in a crisis. You are going to make it through!

God has a plan for your life. Plans to give you a future and plans to give you an expected end. Let me add one more point. *"Expected end"* is a powerful statement and brings this passage to a climax. *"Expected End"* means that God is, and will, fabricate the plot. God is going to create the end that He has for you. That *"End"* is to be prosperous and blessed.

Week Twenty - Four

CRISIS REVEALS WHO YOU ARE

*"**W**herein ye greatly rejoice, though now for a season, if need be, ye are in heaviness through manifold temptations: That the trial of your faith, being much more precious than of gold that perisheth, though it be tried with fire, might be found unto praise and honour and glory at the appearing of Jesus Christ."* 1 Peter 1:6-7

"Beloved, think it not strange concerning the fiery trial which is to try you, as though some strange thing happened unto you." 1 Peter 4:12

"YOU ARE EITHER IN A CRISIS, COMING OUT OF A CRISIS OR GETTING READY TO GO INTO A CRISIS." DR. LESTER SUMRALL

The truth about life is that if you live long enough, you are going to experience seasons of trouble, seasons of trials and seasons of pain. What must we do? We must survive! Every struggle is for a reason and only for a season.

CRISIS CREATES CHANGE... Most people don't change until they are in a season of crisis. Most of those who came to God, came because they couldn't take the pressure of their crisis. The Webster dictionary defines the word, *"crisis"* as *"a turning point in the course of anything."* Crisis is not the end, but the turning point to your next season. God's children are not like the world. There is a greater source living in us that gives us the power to hold up and survive the crisis. Are you in a crisis? Have you thought about quitting? Make up your mind right now that you are going to survive the crisis.

HOW TO SURVIVE:

1. Don't lose sight of the ultimate goal, or you will be incarcerated to the immediate crisis. Keep your focus. The battle is over your focus. God is going to favor you even in a crisis. Start speaking to your future and not to the crisis. Stop telling everyone how bad it is and how awful you have it. Start creating an atmosphere of praise and speak words of faith. Your future is going to materialize.

2. Don't lose sight of your purpose... Remind yourself right now about your purpose. Purpose is stronger than a crisis. Purpose builds passion. God's purpose is to bring you out. Remember, an *expected end*!

3. Elevate in your worship or you will stagnate in your crisis... Learn how to be a worshipper. Worship elevates you. Real worship is unrehearsed. Anyone saved, or not saved, can praise God, but not everyone can worship God. Only those who are connected to Him can worship Him. The best place to be is in the center of unbroken worship. Worship will elevate you to see your life the way God sees it. You will not stagnate, but build for yourself a clearer and broader path to look at when you are raised to a higher level…a higher dimension. You will see the big picture rather than the immediate pain and hurt. Just stop what you're doing, lift your hands and worship! The power of worship is awesome and life changing.

4. There is no fruit that is not bitter before it is ripe. When life throws you lemons, make lemonade. Use what you've been dealt with.

5. The wealth of favor is worship. Get ready to feel the lifting power of God to move into your crisis and to begin accelerating you through it.

You are not going to see this crisis end in despair, but in victory. You are not going to be defeated. You are going to win! You came into this world a winner. You won the most important race of your life when you were just a seed swimming to life. You were the one who pressed harder and pushed faster; out of billions! You have it within you to win! Tap into that inner strength and do it one more time… WIN!

Week Twenty – Five

FAVOR FACTS

"For whoever finds me finds life, and obtains favor from the LORD." Proverbs 8:35 NKJV

He who finds the Lord finds FAVOR. The meaning to the word *"favor"* is "debt cancellation." God says, when you find Him, you have the source that can create the power of wisdom. Wisdom creates the power to cancel debt. Deut 8:18 says, that God has given us the power to get wealth. God gives us that power… I believe God connects us to the right people, to the right job, etc. he who finds the Lord, finds favor!

Would you like to be out of debt? Not just financial, but any debt, until you are free from owing someone something, whatever it is, you are never totally free. You are not really free until you are debt-free. You can't really be free until you have personally experienced the Lord.

Today is the day to discover the power of **FAVOR.**

Jesus worked the law of favor... *"And Jesus increased in wisdom and stature, and in favor with God and man..."* Luke 2:52

Two Kinds of Favor
1. Favor of God
2. Favor of man

Both are very important. Many have tried to preach on the subject of favor, but they usually only preach one side of the truth. Let me give you the whole truth and nothing but the truth. The favor of God is the presence of God in your life. It brings the peace of God. It changes the atmosphere around you; it will ignite a church service.

The most important favor is the favor of God. The favor of God is daily. God is daily sending blessings your way. (Psalm 68:19)

Favor with men is seasonal. God will have to use men to get money to you. The truth about money and increase is that God has never given man one dime. God doesn't make celestial money and send it to you, nor will He enter your atmosphere and give you anything. The real truth is this; God has never handed man one thing. Man could never get that close to God and live.

God never really healed anyone. Now, don't go off the deep end and get all flustered. God is the source to all truth and power, yet, for anyone to be healed, or blessed, they have to follow the instructions given. So, you see, favor with man is important. Prosperity is linked to your connections; the power of godly connections and the power to network are all tied to man. Jesus increased in wisdom and that gave Him favor with God and man.

WISDOM BUILT THE HOUSE OF BLESSING, BUT IT IS FAVOR THAT WILL FURNISH IT.

If you plan to succeed, it will require favor. Favor is nothing more than a season of increase, supernatural connection and timing.

FAVOR NEVER ENTERS YOUR LIFE ALONE...

When favor enters your life so do jealousy and envy. What? You didn't think that favor was free did you? Favor has a price tag on it. Let me help you right now; God doesn't work like Wal-Mart. He's not going to slash the price of favor. You're not going to find favor on a sales rack. It cost what it cost. If you want to be favored, then pay the full price, and get ready for the greatest time of your life. When favor hits it will make no sense.

FAVOR CAN SILENCE A LIFETIME ENEMY...

God favored Mordecai in the book of Esther. Hamon had planned on hanging Mordecai on the gallows, but God favored him. The day Mordecai was supposed to be hung, Hamon was marching him around the kingdom speaking kind words and promotion. Favor can silence a lifetime enemy. Your enemy today will become your servant tomorrow. God gives you an enemy to prepare you for increase. The enemy you conquer determines the reward you will walk in. The size of your enemy reveals the size of your spoils. Having an enemy is sometimes proof that you are doing something right. Favor can silence a lifetime enemy in a day!

FAVOR IS TRANSFERABLE...

We must understand that favor in one person's life can be transferred to another. Joseph transferred his favor to his family. Elijah transferred his favor to Elisha. Only a fool would talk about someone God has favored. Find someone who has been favored, and start recognizing the mantle of favor on their life. You may be thinking, "How do I do that?" Serving is the best way to be allowed in the atmosphere of great men and women.

I have had the privilege of sitting at the table with some highly favored men of God. There have been many times in my life that I would have missed out on my season of favor if I hadn't been willing to sit back and take the servant's role.

FAVOR IS FOR EVERYONE...

Favor is not just a privilege for some people. Favor is a gift for all of us to walk in. You must qualify to increase and walk in favor with God and man. I'm often asked if there are levels of favor. My answer is, yes. The more you grow in wisdom, the more favor you will walk in. Jesus grew in wisdom...He walked in favor with God and man. Get up every day and build your knowledge and claim your favor.

FAVOR IS THE MASTER KEY TO FINANCIAL INCREASE.

No one will succeed in life without favor. Uncommon success will require uncommon favor. You will never advance in your life without the help of those who have already succeeded. There are two kinds of people around you; mentors and friends. A friend usually isn't in a place to help you advance to your next season. A friend loves you the way you are, and mentors love you too much to leave you the way you are. Every time I've changed from one season to another, there were certain mentors speaking into my life that caused me to change. I noticed that my friends began to change when I started to change. My season changed when Dr. Mike Murdock entered my life; so did my friends. Dr. Murdock was so gracious to me and showed me incredible favor. That favor was the master key for me to take up the challenge to write books.

I became a better leader when I began to read John Maxwell's books and became one of his "tape of the month" members. His mentorship was offered to me by the way of reading.

"READERS ARE LEADERS" John Maxwell

FAVOR IS THE GOLDEN KEY TO INCREASE.

FAVOR WILL TURN TRAGEDY INTO TRIUMPH.

FAVOR WILL ACCELERATE YOUR SEASONS OF STRUGGLE.

ONE DAY OF FAVOR IS WORTH A THOUSAND DAYS OF LABOR. Dr. Mike Murdock

Take the time today to notice and proclaim favor over your life. Say this right now, "I am highly favored." Do it! Say it everyday! See if a season of favor doesn't explode in your life. Learn to recognize favor in small things. Declare favor when you get a front row parking space. Declare favor when you didn't have to wait as long as others at the doctor's office. Declare favor when you're standing in line and they open up another register.

Declare Favor Today!

Week Twenty - Six

THE POWER OF PURPOSE

"To everything there is a season, and a time to every purpose under the heaven..." Ecclesiastes 3:1

Y ou will never walk in complete joy and fulfillment until you understand why you are here and why God allowed you to live through what others have died in.

I can not accept that people are here on earth just to work an hourly job, marry, have children, retire and die! There is more to us than just filling time. God has a specific plan for each person alive. Think about this; there is only one of you. There was a divine assignment placed over you the day you were born. Many live life void of understanding their true identity. Could it be that's why counseling is at an all time high? There are so many that seem to be depressed and out of control in churches today.

YOUR TRUE IDENTITY IS REVEALED IN YOUR DIVINE PURPOSE...

I often preach in a youth prison with young men between the ages of thirteen to eighteen.

The first time I ministered there, I began to deal with their purpose, and they began to sit up and listen. This is not a small prison; this is maximum security. They sat there eager and waiting for someone to build the power of hope and purpose in them. I spoke to the hole in their heart and let them know that they matter to God and to me. I told them that God wasn't through with them even though they were living with the mess of their mistakes. They could still turn their life around and fulfill their destiny.

The anointing that destroys the yoke fell in that place and these once hard, staring, mean spirited boys began to melt like wax. Tears started running down their faces as the door of purpose once again, started opening. There was the energy of hope that flooded the room. Purpose destroys despair!

Eighty-five percent of that room stood up without any pulling, or persuading when I gave the altar call for these boys to stand up and be counted for the cause of Jesus Christ; to be adopted into the family of God! Purpose shot through them and change began to manifest immediately.

* **PURPOSE DESTROYS DEPRESSION...**
* **PURPOSE DISPELS INFERIORITY...**
* **PURPOSE PRODUCES THE POWER TO CHANGE...**

*"Who hath saved us, and called us with an holy calling, not according to our works, but according to his own **purpose** and grace, which was given us in Christ Jesus before the world began."* 2 Timothy 1:9

FACTS ABOUT PURPOSE:

PURPOSE REVEALS GOD'S PLAN...

When you discover the purpose of God for your life, God will begin to reveal the plan for your life. You will experience God's true presence once the plan has been revealed. The more your purpose materializes, the more you will experience God's awesome presence. A deeper walk with God is birthed when you understand why you are here and what you are supposed to be doing. Begin to seek the Holy Spirit for your divine purpose when you are spending time with Him in your secret place. When the Holy Spirit begins to unfold the real you, embrace it! All of Heaven's provision is stored up for you in your assignment.

PURPOSE IS ESTABLISHED BY COUNSEL...

"Every purpose is established by counsel..." Proverbs 20:18

GOD'S PURPOSE ALWAYS PREVAILS...

"And the land shall tremble and sorrow: for every purpose of the LORD shall be performed against Babylon, to make the land of Babylon desolation without an inhabitant" Jeremiah 51:29

"This is the purpose that is purposed upon the whole earth: and this is the hand that is stretched out upon all the nations. For the LORD of hosts hath purposed, and who shall disannul it? And his hand is stretched out, and who shall turn it back?" Isaiah 14:26-27

PURPOSE PRODUCES COMMITMENT...

"Who, when he came, and had seen the grace of God, was glad, and exhorted them all, that with purpose of heart they would cleave unto the Lord." Acts 11:23

PURPOSE BRINGS OUT THE GOOD...
"And we know that all things work together for good to them that love God, to them who are the called according to his purpose." Romans 8:28

AN ENEMY CAN PROMOTE YOUR PURPOSE...

"For the scripture saith unto Pharaoh, Even for this same purpose have I raised thee up, that I might show my power in thee, and that my name might be declared throughout all the earth." Romans 9:17

PURPOSE BRINGS US TO HIS WILL...

"In whom also we have obtained an inheritance, being predestinated according to the purpose of him who worked all things after the counsel of his own will." Ephesians 1:11

Week Twenty - Seven

THE RULES OF FAVOR

So many people, when they hear the favor message, immediately assume that it's all about what they can get from God. They assume they can be favored no matter what they do, or say. This is simply not true. One of the dangers of the prosperity message is that we preach the message of sowing without the power of **lifestyle**. Sowing with a seed just to gain money from heaven while your lifestyle doesn't even attempt to please God is no different than playing the lottery. I personally, believe that is out of order and if you are experiencing a return, it doesn't mean that God is pleased with you.

Favor is one of God's greatest gifts to us, but it doesn't come into our lives without a price. There are rules to favor. There is responsibility to living a highly favored life. I was sitting at a conference pondering this chapter in my spirit, when the man of God began to preach. His message shot right through my spirit, as he taught on the word "honor." Honor is very important to God. God says in Malachi 1:6, *"You call me father, but where my honor...is?"* The only commandment with a promise is *"Honor thy father and thy mother and you will live a long life..."*

"...for them that honor me I will honor, and they that despise me shall be lightly esteemed." 1 Samuel 2:30

When we show God honor, He will begin to honor us!

HONOR PRECEDES FAVOR...

Honoring God is first and foremost. You must first understand how to honor God before you can experience His favor. Honor is a reaction; your reactions in life will either honor, or dishonor God.

- What's your reaction to rejection?
- How do you react when you're not getting your way?
- What is your reaction when someone pulls in front of you?
- How do you react when you're standing at a store with twenty-five registers, only two are open and you are in a hurry?
- How do you react to the cashier, to a waiter or waitress?

Does your reaction honor or dishonor God?

HONOR PRODUCES FAVOR...
HONOR PRESERVES FAVOR...
HONOR PROTECTS FAVOR...

If you looked up the word "honor" you would find this definition: *"High regard or great respect given, received or enjoyed... glory, fame, good reputation, credit. A keen sense of right and wrong; adherence to action or principles... chastity or purity..."* Webster New World College Dictionary

REACTION DECIDES YOUR FAVOR...
- Reaction is big to God. I believe your reactions shout louder than your praise.
- Reaction reveals your focus...
- Reaction reveals your intelligence...
- Reaction reveals what's in your heart...
- Reaction to a circumstance decides the longevity of the circumstance...
- Reaction to an offense determines how long the offense stays in your life...

WISDOM DECIDES YOUR LEVEL OF FAVOR...

Wisdom is the factor for every other gift. Favor is given by the wisdom you pursue. The power of knowledge is greater than the force of many. I've heard more than one businessman say, "It's not what you know that is hurting you; it is what you don't know." The difference between lack and prosperity is information. The difference between seasons is information. The difference between a right decision and a wrong decision is information. Labor to build your wealth of knowledge and wisdom, and you will increase your favor.

FOLLOWING AN INSTRUCTION WILL PRODUCE FAVOR...

I labor extra hard to make sure that I follow the instructions of those whom I serve. Dr. Mike Murdock has spent hours teaching me to always have a notepad and to never let those who I am serving have to repeat their instructions. His mentorship has opened many doors. One of the easiest ways to be connected to greatness is to serve it. When you begin to serve, follow the instructions!

FACTS ABOUT FAVOR:

THE POWER OF FAVOR IS WORSHIP...

THE STRENGTH OF FAVOR IS CONNECTION...

THE PROOF OF FAVOR IS PROSPERITY...

THE REASON FOR FAVOR IS TO FULFILL YOUR ASSIGNMENT...

FAVOR CAN TURN TRAGEDY INTO TRUIMPH...

FAVOR CAN SILENCE A LIFETIME ENEMY IN TWENTY-FOUR HOURS...

ONE DAY OF FAVOR IS WORTH A THOUSAND DAYS OF LABOR... (Dr. Mike Murdock)

FAVOR CAN ACCELERATE YOUR SEASON OF STRUGGLE...

FAVOR CAN MAKE YOU WEALTHY IN A SINGLE DAY...

FAVOR NEVER ENTERS YOUR LIFE ALONE...

Week Twenty - Eight

PERFECT PEACE

*"**P**eace be within thy walls, and prosperity within thy palaces. For my brethren and companions' sakes, I will now say, Peace be within thee. Because of the house of the LORD our God I will seek thy good."* Psalm 122:7-9

Peace beyond wisdom... peace that passes understanding... there's a place in God that the mind can't enter; only the heart.

The mind, or intellect, is attached to the flesh. Faith is attached to the heart of believing. There is a season when you have to trust and not understand... step when you can't see... sing when you feel defeated. The enemy is watching your understanding, and hell has no understanding of faith!

Your posture is attached to your faith... Your faith is attached to the power of God's word... Faith comes by hearing the word of faith. The Lord is my refuge. Refuge is a person. In that person, there is a place, in that place, there is a peace, and in that peace, there is a posture of victory, healing, winning and overcoming. I was going through one of the worst seasons in my life when my mentor said to me, "Son, follow your peace..." My first thought was, "What in the world is he talking about? Follow my peace?" After much thought, I realized what was being said. If we have no peace, we can have no focus. Peace brings an atmosphere of joy, praise and focus.

"Let us therefore follow after the things which make for peace, and things wherewith one may edify another." Romans 14:19

HAVING A THANKFUL HEART CAN BRING A SEASON OF PEACE...

That's why they gave a "peace offering" in the Old Testament. They offered up an offering of thanksgiving, and in return, God added peace to the children of Israel.

PLEASING THE LORD BRINGS PEACE WITH YOUR ENEMIES.

"When a man's ways pleases the LORD, he maketh even his enemies to be at peace with him." Proverbs 16:7

THERE IS NO PEACE FOR THE WICKED.

"There is no peace, saith the LORD, unto the wicked." Isaiah 48:22

ORDER PRODUCES PEACE.

"And if the house be worthy, let your peace come upon it: but if it be not worthy, let your peace return to you." Mathew 10:13

Order is the accurate arrangement of things. When your house is in order, there is peace. I have a teenage son, and it seems that one of his friends is always hanging around my house. I asked one of his friends why he always wanted to hang out at my house. His answer was, "There is so much peace in your house." Why is there so much peace? Because my house is in order!

STRENGTH PRODUCES PEACE...

"When a strong man armed keepeth his palace, his goods are in peace." Luke 11:21

JESUS BRINGS PEACE...

"Peace I leave with you, my peace I give unto you: not as the world giveth, give I unto you. Let not your heart be troubled, neither let it be afraid." John 14:27

GOD'S PEACE STOPS THE TROUBLE OF WORRY.

"...Let not your heart be troubled, neither let it be afraid" John 14:27

GODLY INSTRUCTION PRODUCES PEACE...

"These things I have spoken unto you, that in me ye might have peace. In the world ye shall have tribulation: but be of good cheer; I have overcome the world." John 16:33

DOING WELL TO OTHERS BRINGS PEACE...

"But glory, honour, and peace, to every man that worketh good, to the Jew first, and also to the Gentile." Romans 2:10

BEING SPIRITUALLY MINDED PRODUCES PEACE AND LIFE...

"For to be carnally minded is death; but to be spiritually minded is

life and peace." Romans 8:6

SOW PEACE TO REAP PEACE.

"And the fruit of righteousness is sown in peace of them that make peace." James 3:18

You are going to reap whatever you sow! Sow peace, reap peace... sow joy, reap joy...sow money, and reap money!

Week Twenty - Nine

STEPS TO LIVING IN VICTORY

Four steps that will help you successfully walk in the F.O.G. (Favor of God)!

➢ *Make up your mind!*
➢ *Break up your will!*
➢ *Wake up your faith!*
➢ *Take up your cross!*

Make Up Your Mind
"…Choose for yourselves this day whom you will serve…but as for me and my house, we will serve the Lord." Joshua 24:15 NIV

Indecision will stop you from making the advancements it takes to walk in the F.O.G. (Favor of God). You must make up your mind if you are going to possess peace in your life! Decide that you are going to achieve everything that God desires for you to achieve. Decide right now that you will:

1. *NEVER TURN BACK FROM WHERE GOD HAS BROUGHT YOU.*
2. *PURSUE GOD'S TRUTH IN EVERY SITUATION.*
3. *REPLACE ALL OF YOUR BAD HABITS WITH GOOD ONES.*
4. *WALK IN THE LOVE OF GOD CONSTANTLY.*
5. *FORGIVE ANYONE WHO HAS HURT, OR FAILED YOU.*
6. *ALWAYS REMEMBER GOD IS YOUR SOURCE, NOT MEN.*
7. *REFUSE TO QUIT AND YOU WILL NEVER LOSE!*

Break Up Your Will

"And the world is passing away, and the lust of it; but he who does the will of God abides forever." 1 John 2:17

Neither God, nor Satan, will trespass upon your will. Your will is a powerful force. The *"will"* is the empowerment of God in you to choose God, or Satan. You have the power today to choose life, or death, sickness, or healing and Heaven, or hell. (*Deuteronomy 28*)

Break up your will today! Give up everything you are to the Lord. I promise you, this will be the best thing you have ever done. Give God permission to cleanse every part of your life right now. Whatever you walk away from, you have mastered. Whatever you walk towards has mastered you. Walk in the word of God and break up your will.

Take Up Your Cross

"...and anyone who does not take his cross and follow Me is not worthy of Me. Whoever finds his life will lose it, and whoever loses his life for My sake will find it." Matthew 10: 38- 39 NIV

"And He said to them all, if any man will come after Me, let him deny himself, and take up his cross daily, and follow Me." Luke 9:23

Sometimes, this step is the hardest to follow, because as was mentioned earlier, we tend to think that we will never have any more problems after we accept Jesus as Lord of our life.

In the above Scriptures, Jesus was indicating that even though we have been delivered from the curse of sin, there will still be *"things"* in our life that we must deal with on a daily basis (i.e. habits, thoughts, etc.) The *"things"* may be different each day, but the formula remains the same – we must choose to follow Jesus at any cost.

When Jesus speaks of taking up your cross, He didn't mean a literal cross. He was speaking in a two-fold scenario. First, He was saying that we must be willing to follow Him no matter what the cost, or how difficult it becomes. *(He never said that it would be easy – He only said it would be worth it!)*

Secondly, He wanted us to know that salvation was just the beginning of our journey. We become responsible for what we know. In other words, we must carry our "cross" *(what we know)* to others who need to be set free.

Wake Up Your Faith

"Now faith is the substance of things hoped for, the evidence of things not seen." Hebrews 11:1

"But without faith it is impossible to please Him..." Hebrews 11:6

Faith is...

➤ *REACHING OUT INTO NOWHERE...*
➤ *HANGING ONTO NOTHING...*
➤ *UNTIL GOD TURNS IT INTO SOMETHING!*

FAITH IS EXPECTANCY!

Faith is the substance of something hoped for. What do you

desire? Believe right now that you will receive it and start hoping; that is faith.

You woke up your faith when you decided to ask Jesus into your heart. It took faith to believe that the Lord heard you when you asked Him into your heart. It took faith to even make the decision to accept Christ. Every person has been given a measure of faith. No one is found in life without faith. God knew that one day you would need your faith to be awakened! Why not learn how to apply your faith now that you have awakened the greatest potential in your life?

FAITH WILL WORK IF YOU WORK IT!

How do I grow in my faith? Romans 10:17 *says "Faith comes by hearing the word of God..."* The more you study the word of God and listen to what God is saying through His word, the more your faith begins to grow. The size of your faith will determine the size of your miracle. The size of the seed you sow is determined by the size of your faith. The size of your seed determines the size of your harvest. It is all moved by faith! Faith is the hinge that the door of blessing swings open on. Wake up your faith!

You must be patient. Don't expect to become an expert overnight.

Take the time needed to learn all about peace, rest, hope, restoration and salvation. Then allow God to put you back into circulation so that you can affect those who once affected you. God wants to use you in a great way, but it is a process. Gain the knowledge you need by staying in God's presence everyday.

Patience is a weapon that will demoralize your enemy. Never confuse waiting with patience. Patience is resting in your delay... waiting, is when you are worried about your delay.

1 John 4:4 (NIV) says, *"You, dear children, are from God and*

have overcome them, because the one who is in you is greater than the one who is in the world." God is greater than Satan. You have absolute power over him. Never let him intimidate you. He has already lost the battle.

That power is in you by the Holy Spirit. Let the power out, and you will begin packing for your new journey of success and increase! You need to make up your mind, surrender your will to God, awaken your faith and take up your cross daily.

Now that you're ready to release your faith and believe God for your future, pray this prayer with me:

Lord, I surrender all I have to You. I confess You as my Lord. I need You to help me learn of You. Teach me Your ways and show me how to walk in peace and love. Today Lord, I make up my mind to follow You. I command my faith to arise and walk according to Your words. Lord, I want Your will to be done and not mine. I am willing to take up my cross and follow all of Your truths, for Your truth will set me free. I'm Free! I'm Free! I'm Free! Praise Your Holy Name!

Week Thirty

FAVOR SCHEDULES SEASONS FAITH DECIDES FAVOR'S TIMING

W*isdom decides your level of favor... Favor schedule your seasons....* We must understand that faith decides the timing of favor. Protect your faith. Guard it! Build it! Faith is Heaven' currency.

"When God made his promise to Abraham, since there was no on greater for him to swear by, he swore by himself, saying, "I wi surely bless you and give you many descendants." And so afte waiting patiently, Abraham received what was promised." Hebrev 6:13-15 NIV

"By faith Abraham, when called to go to a place he would later receive as his inheritance, obeyed and went, even though he did not know where he was going. By faith he made his home in the Promised Land like a stranger in a foreign country; he lived in tents, as did Isaac and Jacob, who were heirs with him of the same promise. For he was looking forward to the city with foundations, whose architect and builder is God. By faith Abraham, even though he was past age-and Sarah herself barren-was enabled to become a father because he considered him faithful who had made the promise. And so from this one man, and he as good as dead, came descendants as numerous as the stars in the sky and as countless as the sand on the seashore." Hebrews 8-12 NIV

"By faith Abraham, when God tested him, offered Isaac as a sacrifice. He who had received the promises was about to sacrifice his one and only son, even though God had said to him, "It is through Isaac that your offspring will be reckoned." Abraham reasoned that God could raise the dead, and figuratively speaking, he did receive Isaac back from death." Hebrews 11:17-19 NIV

BELIEVE IN THE MIDST OF THE STORM...

Abraham didn't just believe God in times when everything seemed to be okay, or in times of great victories, Abraham believed God when everything was failing. No matter how hard he tried, he couldn't seem to produce a child.

Abraham was in his seventies when God promised him a son. God didn't fulfill his promise to Abraham until he was almost one-hundred years old. As a matter of fact, the word of God says that God waited. God waited until Abraham was as good as dead in his natural potential to produce seed, and Sarah, his wife, had reached the season in her life that she was unable to bear children. Why? Why did God take so long to fulfill His promise? The only answer I can offer is that, He waited so Abraham and Sarah could have no confidence that their flesh could produce anything. He wanted them to completely put their trust in Him. No matter what time He chooses to fulfill His promise, He will fulfill it! God will be faithful to what He has promised. Abraham believed this... he didn't allow his situation to dictate his belief system. He rested on the words of the Lord.

FAITH ISN'T FAITH UNTIL IT PASSES THE TEST OF TIME... the test of difficulties, when there is nothing else left in human abilities.

God took twenty-six years to fulfill a promise to Abraham. God waited until there was no human potential to be factored in. There was no human part in the performance... It wasn't going to happen if God didn't do it. You must be willing to reach seasons of drought and emptiness if God's going to be your source. It's at the time you feel as good as dead, that God will walk into your camp, home, or presence, and give you the very word of encouragement that's going to bring you out and take you into your next season of promotion.

FAITH ISN'T FAITH UNTIL IT PASSES THE TEST OF TIME!

THE RIGHTEOUS LIVE BY FAITH.

By faith, when Abraham was tested and believed God, it was credited to him as righteousness. Get a good grasp of this. Good works, or deeds, do not obtain righteousness. That's not to say that works and deeds aren't a part of the Christian walk. The word of God says that he was credited with righteousness because he took God at His word and nothing, or no one, was going to persuade Abraham otherwise.

CONNECT WITH SOMEONE WHO BELIEVES WITH YOU...

What about Sarah? She not only had to have faith, she had to be the one to carry the seed of promise. Sarah had to enter a higher level of faith. Abraham believed, but Sarah had to conceive it. The word of God says that we need to have faith in our hearts. There is no such thing as head faith; there is only heart faith.

DON'T TRY TO FIGURE GOD OUT... JUST DO WHAT HE SAYS.

There is no way you can understand how God is going to heal your cancer, pay a bill that you have no natural funds to pay, or bring home your child who has been away from the Lord. Your mind doesn't possess the ability to understand God, but your heart does. The spirit of man has the power to believe without understanding how. Sarah had to have the heart to conceive. There are some steps that we have to take in order to walk in our promised blessing.

1. **BELIEVE IT!** *You must first **believe**. That's faith. Faith is <u>now</u>; faith is the substance of things hoped for, and the evidence of things not seen.* Hebrews 11:1

2. **CONCEIVE IT!** You must have Sarah's level of faith. You must be able to **conceive it**. The word *"conception"* comes from the word conceive. Visitors came to Abraham's house one evening and told him that Sarah would be pregnant. When Sarah heard this she laughed, and the Lord asked Abraham, "Why is your wife laughing?" Sarah couldn't conceive it in her mind that she was going to be pregnant. After all, it had been twenty-six years and there was still no promised child. The Lord was going to perform the miracle, but waited another year. He had to get Sarah ready to conceive. Conception is the ability to see your promised blessing and carry it internally.

3. **RECEIVE IT!** When you can **believe it** and **conceive it,** you will be ready to **receive and achieve it.**

Abraham's faith produced a son, Isaac. Isaac's name means **laughter**. You will be filled with laughter when your promise comes no matter how long it takes for God to produce it.

CHANGE IS THE PROOF YOU SURVIVED THE TEST.

When you have survived the test, trust me, your praise and worship will be different. You will become more focused... more intense. God will be the reason you are shouting. I love to watch people who have survived crisis, praise. They have such a different attitude. Don't criticize my praise, if you haven't experienced my pain.

Faith is the power of favor. Abraham was able to go through all that he endured because he believed in something bigger than himself. He had faith in God. He trusted God. God favored Abraham everywhere he went. God will favor you in the same way. Do what Abraham did; you will get what Abraham got. FAVOR!

Take the time necessary to build and increase your faith! Labor to hear the voice of God; study the word of God so, when God speaks you will be sure it is Him. God will never speak contrary to what He has already spoken in His word. (Bible) Faith is built on His word.

Remember, faith is God's currency. Cash in your faith... "Cash in" the currency of faith right now! Believe! Do it! Dare to trust! You're about to enter into a new season!

Week Thirty - One

IT'S TIME FOR GOD'S FAVOR
IT'S TIME TO BE BLESSED

BE THE FAVOR OF GOD TO OTHERS!

It is impossible to help somebody when you are struggling to keep up with your own needs. God has a purpose for you to increase, and it's not just to spend all of your abundance on you. God's chief goal in your life is to make you a blessing to others. God must first bless you to make you a blessing to others. This is the real reason for the F.O.G. (Favor of God)

Others will notice that God's hand is upon you when the favor of God is manifested in your life.

"The Spirit of the Lord God is upon me; because the Lord hath anointed me. . ." Isaiah 61:1

The anointing is God's ability in you to be a deliverer. Stop reading at this moment and shout to the enemy that you are appointed as one of God's deliverers. You are coming out of your crisis today, and you're coming out with great substance. Shout, "I'm blessed Devil, and I'm going to be a blessing to the captives." Shout, "I'm coming out! I'm coming out! I'm coming out of this sickness! I'm coming out of this financial valley of debt! I'm coming out of this relationship problem! My children are coming out! My home is coming out! My children's children are coming out!"

I want to use a phrase that a friend of mine uses all the time when he's blessing someone: "**BE THE F.O.G.**" (favor of God) You can "Be the F.O.G." in someone's crisis. Anytime you help someone out of the pit of despair, anytime you send someone a financial blessing, you have just become the F.O.G.! Wealth is to be used to ease the burden and to break the yoke! When you start to increase, get ready for all of hell to break out against you. Let me ask you a question, if prosperity is of the devil, then why does he attack you so severely when you start to increase? Satan doesn't want you to understand that most of your increase will come from the barns where he has stored what he has stolen. The wealth of the wicked is stored up for the righteous.

Let me encourage you not to panic when you experience a lot of opposition around you. There will be opposition whenever you are breaking through to another spiritual level.

Opposition is a sure sign that God is about to promote you. Attack always precedes promotion.

Attack reveals that Satan is losing hold of your future. This is why he has entered into your present circumstances. He has left your future to attack your present. You're mastering what's been mastering you. Your habits are dying. Things that were holding you down are now falling off of you. You're coming out of your season of madness and are entering into your season of miracles. When you are being raised as one of God's deliverers, you will experience opposition. Get excited when opposition is in your life! You are about to experience your miracle!

Don't ever let someone convince you that God is not interested in increase. The whole reason that God saved you was to bestow on you the privilege of increase. Think for a moment. How can you really be a good representative of God? Are you a good witness when you can't pay your bills on time, or when your children dress in hand-me-down clothes because you can't afford to buy new ones? I don't understand how walking in God's best is not what the average believer thinks is God's plan for them.

God says in His word, *"And Jesus...said...there is no man that hath left house...or lands, for my sake, and the gospels. But he shall receive an hundredfold now in this time."* Mark 10:29-30

The Bible tells us God's plan is to prosper those in His service one-hundred fold. One-hundred fold is abundance. You possess the ability to help someone else out of their storm when you are walking in abundance, and you will be able to tell them that the reason you are blessing them is because God has blessed you. We possess the power to liberate the captives when we walk in the anointing. The anointing sets you apart from those around you. The anointing is, God smearing His ability on you to set others free!

You cannot set anyone free from anything that you haven't been set free from yourself. If you're bound to it, how can you help someone else out of it? If you told God that all you want to do is to sit at His feet, worship Him and never go anywhere, or do anything for Him, He would tell you that you haven't understood what He's all about. He is about affecting others to increase for Him. There is an old song that my mother used to sing, **"My house is full, but**

My fields are empty." The words used to really touch me. In the song, the question is asked by God, *"Who will go and work for Me today? It seems my children all want to sit around my table, but no one wants to work in My fields."* How can we work in His fields if we are always suffering ourselves?

God is blessing you to be someone's deliverer. God desires to pour His abundance into your life. We must understand something about increase. Your level of understanding prosperity will be the level of prosperity that God pours into your life. You must spend the time necessary for you to increase in your understanding of prosperity; it's at that level you will experience increase. God's word says in Proverbs 13:22 *"....the wealth of the sinner is laid up for the just."*

The greatest witness for Christ is when you can help someone out of their pit of despair. For instance, a friend of mine and his wife, were on their way home when they came upon a young woman whose car was broken down beside the road. My friend decided to pull over to help the young lady out. As he offered his assistance, he discovered that all she had was a flat tire. While he was changing the tire, he noticed that all the other tires were bald and needed to be replaced.

BECOME SENSITIVE TO THOSE WHO CAN UNLOCK YOUR FAVOR...

He decided to follow her to make sure she arrived home safely. Once she had gotten home, the woman's worried husband came out. She began to tell her husband what had happened and how my friend had helped her in her time of trouble. Her husband began to thank my friend and his wife. He explained that while he didn't like the fact that his wife was riding on such awful tires, they just didn't have the money to purchase new ones.

My friend and his wife couldn't get the look on that man's face out of their spirit after they left. He turned to his wife and said, "It is a sin if we have the means to meet someone else's needs and don't. We need to go back and help those people out." They did just that.

What a feeling they must have felt, when they pulled up in front of the house, placed five one-hundred dollar bills in an envelope and wrote these words: God is bigger than your problems. He also wrote his name and where he attended church. Here's where the F.O.G. comes in. Those people showed up at his church, and both went to the altar and gave their hearts to Jesus. This was a direct result of my friend being willing to give what he had to help someone in need. He became the F.O.G. (Favor of God) at that moment. That is what a deliverer does. He lifts the burden!

Now, if he had been in a place of financial lack, he would not have been able to bless those people. Instead, he became the F.O.G. (Favor of God) in their life, and God was proclaimed as being bigger than their problem. This is the reason for the F.O.G.; to lift someone's burden.

"And the King shall answer and say unto them, Verily I say unto you, Inasmuch as ye have done it unto one of the least of these my brethren, ye have done it unto me." Matthew 25:40

I believe it's time for us to stand up! Walk in our anointing and begin to affect others for Christ!

"He that spared not his own Son, but delivered him up for us all, how shall he not with him also freely give us all things?" Romans 8:32 It's time to walk in the F.O.G.! **(FAVOR OF GOD)**

Week Thirty - Two

BEGINNING YOUR
JOURNEY OF FAVOR

Decisions are the most powerful tool we have in our daily journey to any success. Everything in life that you are experiencing today was the result of a decision you made yesterday. Good or bad, decisions demand consequences.

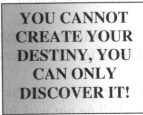

YOU CANNOT CREATE YOUR DESTINY, YOU CAN ONLY DISCOVER IT!

The most important decision you will ever make in life is when you decide to confess Jesus as Lord and walk in the favor of God. The Word of God says in **Romans 10:9** that, "If you confess with your mouth and believe in your heart that Jesus Christ is Lord, you will be saved." By your confession of Jesus as Lord, you have accepted the greatest gift of your life.

This is a time of change and growth for you… To become a Christian, there will be more to this journey than just confessing

Jesus. Fulfilling **Romans 10:9** opens the door to powerful potential and principles that will unlock your next season of life. Up to now, you have been what the church calls, *"lost"*. Not lost, in the sense that you didn't know what you were doing, or where you were... lost, in that you were not walking and fulfilling your spiritual potential.

Destiny is a misunderstood word. The truth about destiny is that you cannot create your destiny, you can only discover it! Now that you are on the right path to discover your true purpose for why you are here on planet earth, get ready for supernatural power and increase to enter your life.

This new decision brings responsibility for you to begin to nurture and grow, so you can make for you, and your family, a season of love, faith and increase.

"For you did not receive the spirit of bondage again to fear, but you received the Spirit of adoption by whom we cry out, "Abba, Father." The Spirit Himself bears witness with our spirit that we are children of God, and if children, then heirs--heirs of God and joint heirs with Christ, if indeed we suffer with Him, that we may also be glorified together." Romans 8:14-17 NKJV

You must understand, with this new found faith, you are now, what we call *redeemed*. You have been set free from past sins and have the power to break every generational curse of your past. You are now walking in a time where you will feel a real sense of God's presence as He begins to bring you into a deeper relationship with Him. However, the reason for this book; is to help you make the proper decisions and steps to confirm and reaffirm your spiritual growth so you can take your place in the army of God.

Jesus came to earth to redeem you from the enemy who has held you in bondage all those years. We praise God that you have been freed from his control! However, this does not mean, that from this day forward, you will not have troubles, or trials. It does mean, however, that you have something greater inside of you than that which held you in the world.

This decision you made doesn't mean that you will not experience any more temptation from the things that you were doing before you decided to follow Christ. It does mean, however, that you now, have a greater power in you to withstand the attacks that held you for so long.

God, the Holy Spirit, is living in you now. He will guide you through the paths you need to take to become what God has predestined for you, if you will allow Him. We will get into a deeper explanation further on in the book.

Week Thirty - Three

QUALITIES
THAT PRODUCE SUCCESS
AND CHANGE

No one likes to arrive at their destination only to learn that important items have been left behind. Have you ever taken a trip, not knowing what the weather would be, only to arrive without the proper clothing? Or, have you ever taken a business trip, and upon reaching the hotel, you realize that you forgot your shoes?

God has given you access to everything you need to make your journey a great success. However, it is your responsibility to gather proper "supplies" in order to be fully equipped for anything that comes your way. There are no shortcuts to **proper preparation.**

PREPARATION ACCOMPLISHES SEVERAL THINGS.
1. Peace of mind.
2. A comfortable journey.
3. The ability to enjoy the scenery along the way.
4. Confidence that you have everything you need.

QUALITIES THAT ARE BENENFICAL:

A RIGHT ATTITUDE

"Let this mind be in you which was also in Christ Jesus..."
Philippians 2:5

The first thing you have to understand is that, you are not the same person you were before you experienced salvation. The devil will try to constantly remind you of everything you used to do, the places you used to go, and who you used to be. He will try to keep you depressed and make you feel that you are not good enough for God's love and mercy. He will try to affect your attitude with negative thoughts.

Be encouraged, and remind yourself daily and constantly, that God's love is totally **UNCONDITIONAL!** Your past has been forgotten and forgiven. The Bible says in Psalm 103:12, *"As far as the east is from the west, so far has He removed our transgressions from us."* God has chosen to forget our past failures and shortcomings because of His love for us. If He chooses to forget our sins, why do we continue to hang on to those things?

The most difficult battle you will ever fight is within yourself! You have to take control of every thought and memory, and remember that you have been delivered from your past.

2 Corinthians 10:4-5 says, *"For the weapons of our warfare are not carnal but mighty in God for pulling down strongholds, casting down arguments and every high thing that exalts itself against the knowledge of God, bringing every thought into captivity to the obedience of Christ."*

CREATE A HUNGER FOR THE WORD OF GOD:

"As newborn babes, desire the pure milk of the Word that you may grow..." 1 Peter 2:2

Just like a baby needs milk to grow strong, you as a new *"spiritual baby"* need to develop a constant diet of the word of God to strengthen your spirit. When you were living by the world's standards, you fed your spirit with "worldly food." Now that you have made the decision to follow Jesus, you need to change your diet.

Imagine that there are two people living inside of you right now – *"Flesh man"* and *"Spirit man"*. Up until this time in your life, you have fed the *"Flesh man"* with a constant diet of everything the world has to offer, while your *"Spirit man"* has been sitting in the corner of your heart starving to death and weak. Now, it is up to you to turn the tables on these guys!

This change will not come naturally, or easily. The *"Flesh man"* is going to fight you for the things you were used to eating. At first, you will have to make a conscious decision to hunger for the word of God. However, the more you feed the *"Spirit man"* the stronger he will grow and the easier it will become to eat the right 'food'.

WORK ON YOUR HABITS:

"Therefore, if anyone is in Christ, he is a new creation; old things have passed away; behold, all things have become new." 2 Corinthians 5:17

Scientists have proven that anything you do for twenty-one days will become a habit. You have probably found this to be true even before you became a Christian. The same principle holds true in God's Kingdom.

Just like all of us, before you made a commitment to Jesus

Christ, you struggled with bad habit, such as anger, bitterness, depression, addictions to drugs, alcohol and tobacco, sexual perversions, or any of a multitude of others. You may still be struggling with some bad habits even now. This is not uncommon – God didn't ask you to clean yourself up in order to come to Him; all He asks is for you to come as you are – He'll do the cleaning!

We must make the effort to change our habits in order to move forward. We must replace the bad habits with good ones, such as, prayer, Bible study, church attendance, fellowship with other believers, tithing and seeding, faith, love for people, mercy etc.

Sometimes, it is not easy to change our habits. We become so entangled by them that we don't realize that they exist in our lives. We must rely on those around us to help us to change. That is why it is so important for you to surround yourself with the right people. This leads us to another important step on your journey:

SEEK GODLY MENTORSHIP:

"Wisdom is the principal thing; therefore get wisdom. And in all your getting, get understanding." Proverbs 4:7

You are entering into a critical area in your walk with God. There are many things that you will need to know in order to be successful and victorious in your quest to follow God's path for you. Although you can make progress on your own, you will avoid many pitfalls and obstacles, by seeking mentorship from godly people. Your spiritual development will move much more quickly when you align yourself with someone who has already gone through the trials and struggles and moved into a victorious, overcoming life with the Lord.

We will touch on this a little later, but you need to find a local church body that you can become a part of to begin your growth process. You need to make sure that the church is biblically sound and preaches the whole word of God. It is essential that they teach about the power of the Holy Spirit, restoration and evangelism. They need to emphasize the current operation of spiritual gifts within the believer, as this will be your arsenal of warfare power. Also, the principles and laws of seeding and harvest need to be taught and in operation within the body of believers you choose to worship alongside.

There are many people you can seek out for mentorship. First, and foremost, is your Pastor. He has been assigned by God to shepherd the flock through sound teaching, training and equipping. Mentorship can also come through godly friends and family. There are many great books, tapes and videos by anointed men and women of God that will give you instruction and inspiration. Find someone that you can trust to make you accountable for areas in your life that you are struggling with, and maintain contact with them in order to eliminate temptations that may occur. Always remember, there is strength in numbers!

DESIRE GODLY FELLOWSHIP

Don't wait for your mentor to find you. Seek them out. Absorb their counsel, apply it to your life and watch how quickly change takes place.

"And let us consider one another in order to stir up love and good works, not forsaking the assembling of ourselves together, as is the manner of some, but exhorting one another, and so much the more as you see the Day approaching." Hebrews 10:24- 25

As was mentioned earlier, it is essential that you find a good, Bible-believing church in which to worship. You may already have a church home and just need to get "plugged in" to the fellowship. You may be a brand new Christian and have no godly friends. In either case, you probably were surrounding yourself more with non-believers, than believers. You need to break your ties with worldly associations at this time in your walk.

We are not trying to say that you have to be hateful to them, or create problems in your workplace. As long as you are alive, there will always be those around you who will not want to live for God. When you get stronger in your faith, these will be your instant "mission field" for sharing the love of Jesus, so you don't want to "tick them off" What I'm trying to get across is that, as a "spiritual babe" in Christ, you need time to strengthen your own walk before you try to change others.

There is no better way to find good, Christian fellowship than in church. Find one that is preaching a relevant and practical word, operates in the power of the Holy Spirit, walks in the anointing of the gifts of the Spirit and one that believes and actively participates in the principles and laws of seeding and harvest. You should also find a fellowship that is outreach oriented and ministers beyond the four walls of the church.

Let the Holy Spirit give you guidance as you pray about and seek out your place of worship.

AN ENEMY IS NECESSARY:

"Be sober; be vigilant; because your adversary the devil walks about like a roaring lion, seeking whom he may devour." 1 Peter 5:8

The first thing we are told in the above passage of scripture is, to be *"sober"*. The writer is trying to say that we need to have a clear mind and be alert. Our minds must be in order and clear to be able to recognize the attack of the enemy. The biggest battle you will ever fight will be in your own mind. I highly recommend that you get a copy of the book, ***The Battlefield of the Mind*** by, Joyce Meyer. It will help you to understand that your mind will be the first place the enemy will attack. If he can get your mind imbedded with negative thoughts, remembrances of your past and improper ideas, he has already won the battle. When Satan approached Eve in the garden, his strategy was to appeal to her intellect. The questions he asked her were those that were thought provoking. Why did he use this tactic? He knew that a person's life will move in the direction of their most dominant thoughts. *Proverbs 23:7* says, *"For as he thinks in his heart, so is he..."* This is one of the most important and most basic lessons in life – WE ARE WHAT WE THINK!

"Finally, brethren, whatsoever things are true, whatsoever things are honest, whatsoever things are just, whatsoever things are pure, whatsoever things are lovely, whatsoever things are of good report; if there be any virtue, and if there be any praise, think on these things." Philippians 4:8

Your mind is the birthplace of everything you do. Satan knows this. His greatest weapon is to get you to break your focus on God's plan for your life. It's been said that, most people fail in life because of broken focus. Satan is out to sabotage your focus in order to abort your godly assignment. So, you can see how important it is to guard your thoughts well.

The next thing 1 Peter 5:8 tells us is to be "vigilant." Webster's dictionary defines vigilant as *"staying watchful and alert to danger or trouble."*

Peter knew that we would face the same attack of the enemy trying to gain a foothold in our minds because of his own struggles in this area. A small foothold will turn into a stronghold in your life if you are not watchful and prepared. A foothold can be removed far easier than a stronghold. Satan's main goal is to destroy what God is doing in you, so stay alert!

There will never be a time in your life when you won't have an enemy. Having an enemy is not all bad – the size of your enemy will determine the size of the reward awaiting you. You need to understand that when opposition comes – and it will – it is coming in proportion to the increase of your understanding of who you are in Christ. As you grow, affliction will grow. As affliction grows, the grace of God will increase to help you overcome. After the attack is over, you will find that whatever strength your enemy possessed will be implanted into your life.

When Satan launches an attack in your life, it will very often come through a person. The sad thing is, most times, the people he uses will usually be someone close to you (i.e. a family member, spouse or close friend!) Keep in mind that, your enemy, is anyone who attempts to stop the will of God from being fulfilled in your life. Not everyone will understand what God is doing in you. You must identify and move away from anyone who breaks your focus on God's plan for you. Stay away from the spirit of strife and confusion. Don't lend an ear to people who try to stir up trouble. Guard yourself and trust in God. And always remember:

"You, dear children, are from God and have overcome them, because the one who is in you is greater than the one who is in the world." 1 John 4:4 (NIV)

You never need to be afraid of any enemy that comes against you. Satan was defeated at Calvary by the shed blood of Jesus! Don't panic when you see an attack coming your way. Be ready! Take the offensive! Destroy it quickly!

How to keep your mind clear and ready for battle:

*"Do not conform any longer to the pattern of this world, **but be transformed by the renewing of your mind**. Then you will be able to test and approve what God's will is – His good, pleasing and perfect will."* Romans 12:2 (NIV)

MAKE PRAYER A PRIORITY
"Be anxious for nothing, but in everything by prayer and supplication, with thanksgiving, let your requests be made known to God." Philippians 4:6

Simply stated, prayer is communication with God. However, you will find that the more you dedicate yourself to prayer, the communication evolves into communion and communion builds into relationship. We all desire to have loving, lasting relationships with those whom we love and who love us. **Nobody loves you more than the One who created you.** *Nobody wants you to succeed more than God.* God longs for you to desire Him and live in full blessing and increase spiritually, mentally and physically. However, we will never know how much He really loves us without developing a consistent prayer life.

Nothing is more important than knowing God's will for your life. The only way to find that will is by spending quality time talking with Him on a daily basis. The Bible tells us that, David was a man after God's own heart. In Psalm 42, David writes that, there is a place you can reach in your prayer life, where prayer becomes a continual, twenty-four-hour-a-day, seven-days-a-week, relationship. Through prayer, you get to know the nature of God. You will also begin to see the bigger picture of His plan and how you fit into what He is doing at this moment all over the world.

2 Timothy 2:15 (KJV) says, *"Study to show thyself approved unto God..."* A vital part of learning about God is through prayer. It is good to read about God, but why not talk to the source? You will find new doors of understanding and opportunity unlocked and waiting for you to walk through for complete victory as you make prayer a priority in your life.

ALLOW TIME FOR CHANGE TO HAPPEN

"But let patience have its perfect work, that you may be perfect and complete, lacking nothing." James 1:4

"But we all, with unveiled face, beholding as in a mirror the glory of the Lord, are being transformed into the same image from glory to glory, just as by the Spirit of the Lord." 2 Corinthians 3:18

One of the hardest things to learn is to be patient and allow God to transform your life into what He wants you to be. Waiting and patience is lacking in our society today. We want instant gratification and quick answers. One of the biggest lies Satan tries to perpetrate against you is that God has forgotten you. It is true, that when you ask Jesus to be Lord of your life, God can instantly deliver you and set you free from habits, addictions and attitudes. I wish it were that easy in every situation, but you must understand, some situations take time. Remember, you didn't get into your problems overnight, so you have to be willing to give God time to bring total deliverance to you. It may come quickly, or it may come slowly. The only guarantee He gives is, that it will come!

Keep your focus on growing and maturing in your understanding as the process unfolds. Don't sit idly by and do nothing. Keep in mind the familiar saying, "an idle mind is the devil's workplace." Stay focused on prayer... Start getting to know God's specific purpose for your life. Surround yourself with people who will encourage and edify your spirit. Always remember, a victorious lifestyle is a process – every movement forward is progress. As Paul said in *Philippians 3:14 (KJV)*, *"keep pressing toward the mark for the prize."*

DEVELOP A LIFESTYLE OF *GIVING LACED WITH EXPECTANCY* FOR A *HARVEST*

"Give, and it will be given to you; good measure, pressed down, shaken together, and running over will be put into your bosom. For with the same measure that you use, it will be measured back to you." Luke 6:38

The Bible is a book of promises. Every page tells us about the goodness of God to His children. One thing that God cannot do is, lie. He also cannot fail! If He promised it, He will do it!
However, with every promise, there will be a condition. The one thing God needs from us is our willingness to allow Him the opportunity to operate in our lives. We must act first in the prerequisites that God has established through His Word in order

to be blessed and live in victory and increase.

The above scripture says that, in order to receive the best God has for us we must first, give our best for Him. It also says that, God is going to give to us in direct proportion to what we give to Him!

"Will a man rob God? Yet you have robbed Me! But you say, 'in what way have we robbed You?' In tithes and offerings... 'Bring all the tithes into the storehouse, that there may be food in My house, and try Me now in this,' says the Lord of hosts, 'if I will not open for you the windows of Heaven and pour out for you such blessing that there will not be room enough to receive it. And I will rebuke the devourer for your sakes, so that he will not destroy the fruit of your ground, nor shall the vine fail to bear fruit for you in the field,' says the Lord of hosts." Malachi 3:8, 10-11

Now, the tithe was established from the beginning. God set the law of the tithe for our benefit. You will find protection, health and blessing within the law of the tithe; the enemy is rebuked in exchange for the tithe. Tithe simply means "tenth." We are responsible to give the FIRST ten percent of our increase back to God in order for the "windows of Heaven" to open. This is non-negotiable. Do not expect God to do anything in your life if you refuse to operate within His law. Giving offerings as seed is over and above the first ten percent. The tithe is required to go into the "storehouse" (your home church), but the seed, or offering, can be given to anything you feel God leading you to pour into. The only caution we could give is, make sure that you are planting into "good soil." That is between you and God.

Increase and blessing in your life is a promise when you operate within God's law of tithe and seed! God says to test Him, and see if He will not hold true to His Word. Remember, He CANNOT lie!

Make giving of your best – not only financially, but in time and service – a continuous lifestyle. The results will blow you away!

Week Thirty - Four

THE RIGHT PATH TO OBEDIENCE

"You shall not make idols for yourselves; neither a carved image nor a sacred pillar shall you rear up for yourselves; nor shall you set up an engraved stone in your land, to bow down to it; for I am the LORD your God. You shall keep My Sabbaths and reverence My sanctuary: I am the LORD. If you walk in My statutes and keep My commandments, and perform them, then I will give you rain in its season, the land shall yield its produce, and the trees of the field shall yield their fruit. Your threshing shall last till the time of vintage, and the vintage shall last till the time of sowing; you shall eat your bread to the full, and dwell in your land safely. I will give peace in the land, and you shall lie down, and none will make you afraid; I will rid the land of evil beasts, and the sword will not go through your land. You will chase your enemies, and they shall

fall by the sword before you. Five of you shall chase a hundred, and a hundred of you shall put ten thousand to flight; your enemies shall fall by the sword before you. For I will look on you favorably and make you fruitful, multiply you and confirm My covenant with you. You shall eat the old harvest, and clear out the old because of the new. I will set My tabernacle among you, and My soul shall not abhor you. I will walk among you and be your God, and you shall be My people. I am the LORD your God, who brought you out of the land of Egypt, that you should not be their slaves; I have broken the bands of your yoke and made you walk upright. Leviticus 26:1-13 NKJV

Two paths are opened up for us in this chapter, one path, is a path of obedience and blessings follow. The other path is a path of disobedience and curses are the result.

Let's take a look at the path of obedience, understanding, that if we don't obey, we can expect a season of pain and suffering. My focus here is to motivate you to live a life of obedience to God.

CHARACTERISTICS OF THE OBEDIENT:

The obedient will have no idols. (Vs. 1) An idol is anything you place before God. Whatever is placed before God angers Him. This means that we cannot place our kids, our careers, our hobbies, etc, before Him.

Reverence the appointments of God. (Vs. 2) The obedient never trivialize the presence and appointments of God. Those, who are obedient, will not turn the Lords day into a day of selfish pleasure, or desecrate the things of God, His church, His people, or His ministers.

The obedient are guided by His Word. (Vs. 3) They walk in the statues of the Lord. To the obedient, the Word of God is the final word. There is no questioning His truth. They base every decision on what God says, or has said, about it.

They delight to do His will. (Vs. 3) The Word of God is to be kept. This is the code of conduct for the obedient. Not as the miser keeps his money, hoarded to be useless, but as a warrior keeps his sword. The obedient are not just about hearing the truth, but they are about doing it.

BLESSINGS THAT ACCOMPANY THE OBEDIENT:

Fruitfulness (Vs. 4) Then I will give you rain in due season. This promise is conditional. Fruitfulness depends on our relationship with God, where all fruit is found. The vine gives the branch the life substance that produces fruit. The closer we are to God, the more fruit we will reap.

Peace and Rest (Vs. 6) the secret of fruitfulness and restfulness is being calmly obedient to God's will.

Deliverance from evil things (Vs. 6) there are many beasts, and enemies lying in wait to devour us. God promises us a life of safety and security when we are obedient to His Words. God is able!

Power to Overcome (Vs 7, 8) in spiritual warfare, it's not about numbers and strength. It's not about experience, but it is about holiness. It is weak things the Lord uses to defeat the strong.

Never walking alone (1 Cor. 1: 26 – 31) It doesn't matter how much money you don't have… or power… or might… What does matter is who is going with you. The obedient are guaranteed that they won't be alone.

Distinguishing Favor (Vs. 9) Never seek the favor of men, always seek the favor of God. God's favor is far more valuable than mans. Favor is a major necessity for being successful. The obedient are guaranteed favor, not just favor, but distinguishing favor. This means you're not lucky, you are favored!

Abundant Provision (Vs. 10) Old blessings will not have to be hoarded because of the number of new ones that keep showing up. Everything we use will not run out. He is a God that is more than enough! The obedient, will walk in incredible provision.

Provision, is something scheduled for your future that, is revealed in what is hidden in your today.

Divine Fellowship (Vs. 12) His presence is protection, prosperity, progress, purity, and power. The person, who walks according to God's laws, walks upright before Him and has His presence abiding with them and around them. Greater is the Spirit of Christ in us, than the spirit of the anti-Christ which is around us.

Make it your main decision this week to become an obedient believer.

Week Thirty - Five

IT IS FINISHED!

So when Jesus had received the sour wine, He said, "It is finished!" And bowing His head, He gave up His spirit." John 19:30 NKJV

First, let's make it clear that, this phrase doesn't mean what you think it means, yet it does. It's not just finished, something has also begun. The phrase that Jesus' spoke here has a three fold meaning. It should read like this. It *is* finished, it *was* finished and it *shall be* finished. A more modern way to say it would be, "MISSION ACCOMPLISHED."

It doesn't mean defeat, but victory. It doesn't mean the end, it means the beginning. This phrase has a past, present, and future tense power. When the enemy heard this statement he shook from head to toe.

PAST TENSE:

In third person, one speaks for another. When Jesus said this, He was first speaking in third person. He was speaking for the Father. He was declaring, "Father, your plan is completed, it's done, it's finally finished." What plan? It was God's plan to bring mankind back into right relationship with Him, not just for Jews, not just for one nation, but for everybody who confesses and believes in the Lord Jesus Christ.

Jesus is speaking with divine authority. On the cross, He's not speaking as Mary's son. He's not speaking as a human. He's speaking as, the High Priest, the Son of God, the sacrificial Lamb. He's speaking as the Alpha, and the Omega, the Beginning and the End. He's speaking as the Bright and Morning Star.

There will be NO MORE! No more blood offerings will ever have to be lifted up again. The God of Heaven will redeem mankind. Their sins will be forgiven, not just covered up. When Jesus said "IT IS FINISHED" God rent the veil that had for years, kept Him separated from His people. The Sins of Adam and Eve were now paid in full and all of mankind through Jesus, has access to God.

PRESENT TENSE:

Present tense means a state of action. Jesus was speaking for Himself. He was declaring that what He came to do, His suffering, His pain, and His punishment for sins He didn't commit, were now over. It is finished! He was going home. Heaven was His focus. Jesus left the splendor of heaven to walk as a mortal man, so He could become the first of many to overcome.

Jesus shed His blood seven times.
1. At the Garden of Gethsemane…
2. When He was beaten by the Jews.
3. Whcn He was scourged by the Romans.
4. When they put the crown of thrones on His head.
5. On the way to Calvary.
6. When they nailed Him to the cross.

7. When the Roman soldier pierced His side with the spear and blood and water flowed.

Jesus was declaring that, He had fought a good fight, He had kept the faith, He had been weighed and tried, but He was not found wanting.

FUTURE TENSE:

God died for your future success. When Jesus said, "It is finished" He was also speaking to the walls that have been built in your future. He was speaking in all three dimensions as the same, yesterday, today and forever.

Your future is secure in Christ because He has already been there before you.

Week Thirty - Six

FIVE SECRETS
TO A
FAVORED WEEK

SECRETS TO WALKING IN HAPPINESS:

Sooner or later, most of us arrive at a time in our lives when we say, "**Something is wrong!**" It can happen to anyone at any time, or at any age. Different circumstances –a not especially – welcomed birthday, a child going to college – The circumstances are not the problem. The circumstances simply shine the light on it. The discomfort or unhappiness you feel comes from within.

CIRCUMSTANCES DON'T MAKE US THEY REVEAL US.
We all want peace with who we are, and what we are doing. These five insights can help you find that peace and lasting happiness. Peace and success comes from within. When you are in crisis, don't go back to sleep, wake up! Stand still! See what God is about to do for you!

CHANGE YOUR GOALS:

Sometimes, all we need to do is evaluate our goals. Changing your goals can send a message to your brain that your life is still moving forward in the midst of your crisis. Have you ever been told, "If you set your mind to it, you can achieve anything"? I believe this to be possible, but I also believe that, failure will be part of your achieving. The problem with happiness is that we have tried to attach our feelings of worth and self-acceptance to our external success. If what you're doing is not working, simply change your goals. *If you don't like your harvest, change your seed.* Failure is not what we are; failure is what we have tried to do. Don't attach failure to your self-worth; we have all failed at some time in our attempts to succeed. Happiness is not attached to what I do; it is attached to who I am and to whom I serve. His name is Jesus.

CHANGE THE WAY YOU SEE YOURSELF:

You will never rise above your own self-image. You will never out perform your own self-likeness. See yourself the way God sees you and not the way others see you. *"...For I am fearfully and wonderfully made; Marvelous are your works...* (Psalm 139:14 NKJV) Make this your last day wishing you had someone else's equipment. You are made to do something unique. Your difference is where your value exists. Find your difference and you will become more joyous. When we find our own self-worth, we tend to stop competing with others. This alone will produce happiness.

COMMIT TO YOUR UNDERSTANDING THAT THERE IS A DIFFERENCE BETWEEN PLEASURE AND HAPPINESS:

Pleasure cannot be sustained beyond the experience producing it; whether it's from something we do, eat, or have. Pleasure lives in our external world. Thus, if we are not being fed what causes us pleasure, we tend to become depressed, discouraged and unhappy. Too much of the outside world causes us to become phony and we lose our own self-identity that lives inside of us. If we base our happiness on pleasure, we will always come up short. But when we base our happiness on what we are... Our faith, our commitments, and our character, we will always come out on top.

STOP BEING A TAKER AND START BEING A GIVER:

Learn that the more you help others, the less you have time to self-evaluate all your mistakes. Use your losses as your message to help raise someone else to their goals. Make sure that those you help qualify for your instructions. Qualify every relationship, and when you find someone who has qualified for your love, your caring, your joy, then guess what, give it. Giving is the quickest way to destroy unhappiness. Watching someone rejoice over what you did for them can be like medicine to your soul.

HAPPINESS IS THE REWARD FOR DISCERNING THE RIGHT VOICE IN YOUR LIFE:

Your future and happiness is decided by the voice you choose to listen to. That's why I labor to hear the voice of the Holy Spirit everyday. He's the only person in my life and yours that knows exactly what has been placed inside of you. Thus, He will never require something from you that you are unable to do. The Bible calls the Holy Spirit, your Comforter, your Counselor, and your Guide. He's the one who walks beside you everyday. Stop ignoring the most important person in your life. Your happiness is attached to Him.

Week Thirty - Seven

HOW TO WALK IN FINANCIAL FAVOR

MONEY GEARS

Have you ever noticed when you are driving your car, that there is a first, second, and sometimes third gear below the letter "D" that stands for "Drive"? "D" is the best gear you can drive in. "D" offers you the maximum ability to drive at the maximum speed. "D" or "Drive" is the position that causes you to accelerate to your destiny with quicker accuracy.

MAKING MONEY:

First gear is a mind-set that we've all been inundated with. It's the mind-set of, MAKING MONEY. We have all been taught that the first step to increase is to first make money. Our parents and society, begin imprinting these images on our minds at an early age. That image, reminds us that, if we want something, we have to make money to get it. So, we buy into the philosophy of getting a job, being paid hourly, and every week take the money we've made and spend it on what we want. Then, on Monday morning, we get up, and again, repeat the process of making money. Now, if we never change gears, we sure won't move very fast and staying in first gear too long will eventually burn out your transmission; yes, we will move forward in first gear, but think how long it's going to take to arrive at your destination. Come on, let's shift to second gear.

MANAGING MONEY:

Second gear is when we begin to start managing the money we are now making. There tends to be a different concept in the mind of those who start managing their money, instead of just spending it. One, who manages, is usually in charge of a group of people. Managing your money is when you now control your money and your money no longer controls you. Money makes a terrible master, but a wonderful servant. Let's shift to third gear.

MOVING MONEY:

In third gear, we find that money is best used when it is moving. Its very name "currency" indicates movement. Money was never meant to sit around and do nothing. Money is a tool! Money is the key to more money. Have you ever heard someone say, "It takes money to make money"? This is so true. If I want to be on more television stations; then guess what, I have to be willing to spend more money. This is why giving is a part of increase. Giving, or sowing your money, is keeping your money moving. I can't think of a better investment for your money than in the Kingdom of God.

MULTIPLY MONEY:

In over-drive, you are going to begin to experience the power of accelerated increase. My good friend, Dr. Todd Coontz, of Coontz Investment, shared with me, that the most powerful tool we have is placing our money in a compound interest savings. Over time, your money can grow and you're earning interest on interest money, as well as, the money you place in savings. Consult a financial advisor. Your local bank can offer you a savings account, but they usually give very low interest rates.

MY TOP TEN STAYING OUT OF DEBT KEYS:

1. *Buy only what you need, not what they're selling.*
2. *Never compete with others around you.*
3. *Move your furniture around, clean your car, and repaint the walls. Sometimes this is all that's needed to make you feel better about what you already have.*
4. *Research your purchases before you buy. You don't have to purchase brand name equipment to acquire good quality.*
5. *"Take care of your shop and your shop will take care of you." Benjamin Franklin*
6. *Don't charge what you can't pay off in 30 days.*
7. *Never pay minimum payments on your credit cards.*
8. *Pay your tithes. Yes, I said pay your tithes, as a matter of fact; pay them off the top of your gross, not the net. Tithing will get God involved in your finances.*
9. *Wait 24 hours before you purchase big items. Sleep on it. Sometimes you will discover that you can wait.*
10. *Remember, want is stronger than need. Never trade off your needs for something you want. Stick to a spending plan.*

Week Thirty - Eight

CONFIDENCE IS STRONGER THAN STATURE

When David approached his nemesis, named, Goliath, it wasn't David's size, or stature that intimidated the enemy, it was his confidence. Think for a moment. Here's a young boy facing a skilled warrior. David wasn't even dressed like a champion. He was dressed like the shepherd boy that he was. Just because we appear to be something else to others, doesn't mean we aren't who God has predestined for us to be. You don't have to look like a champion to be one. Being a champion is far greater than just looking like one. David's confidence in His God gave him the confidence to face his enemy and not just face him, but defeat him! It wasn't David's stature that allowed him to conquer Goliath, it was his confidence...his knowledge that he, with God, would overcome.

I believe that one of the greatest attacks on the body of Christ is an attack on our confidence. With so much pain, crisis and loss, we've begun to believe the devil's lie that we should accept our life as it is and not try to change it. The enemy is after our confidence. I have five great anointed words for you this month. Are you ready? THE DEVIL IS A LIAR! By the end of this article, you are going to sit up and begin to reclaim lost potential... lost income... lost hope. God is about to give you an Isaiah 55: anointing. He's going to supply seed to the sower and bread to the eater!

Confidence is a belief in your own abilities and talents without comparing yourself with everyone else.

YOU WILL NEVER OUT-PERFORM YOUR OWN SELF IMAGE!

When you compare yourself to someone else, you'll always come up short in comparison. Why? Because you always compare your weaknesses to their strengths...*Self confidence is the key ingredient to a healthy and healed life.*

"Never bend your head. Always hold it high. Look the world straight in the face."-Helen Keller

I love this quote...Helen Keller challenges us in this quote to look the world straight in the face, build up our confidence and never hang our heads as though we are lower than our worth, and to always hold our head high to see our glorious God-given destiny. Be proud of who you are! No matter what life deals you, you can achieve and will succeed!

Helen Keller was deaf, mute, and blind, but her confidence was not built on her physical weakness, but on her mental ability to realize that her identity was based on what she could become. For Helen Keller to become the woman she became, someone had to mentor her...show her that there was more to Helen Keller than just being able to see, hear, and speak. If we are to succeed, we are going to have to overlook our weaknesses and begin to build our **confidence,** believing that there is more to us than just our basic abilities. Stop waiting for others to identify you, and recognize that you have to build your confidence. Confidence is not built on what others think. Confidence is built on what you think about yourself first. "For as a man *thinks* in his heart, so is he..."

Lack of self confidence is one of the greatest problems we face in this country. No wonder we've made Hollywood our example. We've made those who drive nice cars, live in big houses, and have lots of money, the focal point of what we believe to be, genuine success. This is not reality. Many of the well-to-do have more heartaches and depression than those who have very little. Material things were never meant to create real happiness. Real success places value on attributes such as honor, integrity, love, God, and a secure and happy home.

"I rejoice therefore that I have confidence in you in all things." 2 Corinthians 7:16

ENEMIES THAT DESTROY OUR CONFIDENCE:
- Insecurities
- Inadequacies
- Low self-esteem
- Fear
- Bitterness
- Inferiorities
- Relational hurts

All of these can damage your confidence and your hope of a better life. Hope is what faith is built on. Self-confidence leads to self-realization and will produce a healthy self-image. When we lack a good healthy confidence in ourselves, we begin to develop hopelessness and a spirit of "why bother." Have faith in your own abilities. You cannot be successful, or happy, if you don't have confidence in your own powers and abilities. People, who haven't developed their identity, become dependant upon others to qualify them to feel accepted and needed. This attitude will always exhaust the other person in the relationship. No one is capable of supplying what you need every single day. If you are a person in constant need of being be told that you're pretty...that you're okay...that you're successful, and those you depend upon to do so do not supply you with the affirmations, or compliments you need, you'll reproach them for not making you feel good about yourself.

God designed us to draw our strength, love, and acceptance from the Holy Spirit. He is the person who will never leave you. Until you are comfortable with yourself in God, you will always compromise. Compromise will always satisfy religion and avoid a true relationship with God. The sign of compromise is always disloyalty.

Your confidence is a feeling. Feelings of confidence, depends on what kind of thoughts you're allowing to run through your mind. Your ears are the furrow to the soil of your mind. The voice you listen to will determine your future. If you don't control your mind, you will never be able to build a healthy confidence. Begin to fill your mind with pleasant thoughts throughout your day. Stop feeding your pain. Stop feeding your wounds. Allow your pain to create in you a passion to relieve the pain of others. Change your focus. Fill your mind with thoughts of faith, confidence, and security. This will begin to expel those thoughts of negativity and fear.

FIGHT THE SPIRIT OF FEAR:

Fear is the most deadly of all spirits. Fear will paralyze the greatest of men. Fear, is the reason so many fail to change. It keeps them in their prison of doubt and low self-esteem. Dr. Morris

Cerullo, preaches about the one demon spirit that can be the doorway for all the other spirits to enter by. He calls this, "The spirit of terror"... "The spirit of torture" is the SPIRIT OF FEAR. *"Do the thing you fear and the death of fear is certain."* -Ralph Waldo Emerson

Fear never just leaves, it has to be conquered. To conquer fear, you simply have to face what you fear. Stop allowing fear to stop your change and control your life.

Fear will paralyze you from stepping into God's plan for your life. One of the reasons so many believers are living a life of defeat and lack, is fear. The feeling of fear in them is stronger than the spirit of faith. The reason so many walk away from the power of God is the lack of trusting God in times of crisis.

For God hath not given us the spirit of fear; but of power, and of love, and of a sound mind. 2 Timothy 1:7

There are two kinds of fear. For instance, **to fear the Lord**, is the beginning of wisdom, that's healthy fear. What we must understand is that fear will never actually leave us. Fear, used with wisdom, is God's built-in questioning tool to help us be sure. But once you know and have become confident that God is behind your decision then you must face fear and conquer it with your faith. Faith doesn't work without trust. The second kind of fear is **timid fear.** This is the fear that was imprinted in you while you were learning to become an adult. This fear is not from God, nor can it do anything to drive you to God. This fear lives in the closet of your failures... in the bedrock of what others have said to you when you were a child. This demon found a foothold and now has made it a stronghold. This is the fear that stops the flow of favor. This is the demon that has been killing your confidence. God has given us clear instructions through Paul. God did not give us this spirit of fear, but He has given us power! Love! A sound mind!

Fear will cause you to stop believing in miracles.
Fears will hinder your faith walk.

Faith requires the ability to step out, where fear is screaming "No!" Trust, believes God will do what He said after you've stepped out. Fear stops many of us from sowing the seeds that could unlock our lack and poverty.

Let's get in agreement that you are going to conquer the spirit of fear. That you are going to stop listening to the enemy and start listening to God's Word. Your confidence is at stake. Fight the good fight of faith!

FACTS ABOUT CONFIDENCE:

- Confidence creates a peaceful mind-set...
- Confidence is proof you have faith in your future.
- Confidence is proof you've conquered fear.
- Confidence is proof you believe in God's Word.
- Worry is confidence in your adversary.
- Your confidence can open doors.
- Confidence produces the ability to take a chance.
- Confidence creates boldness in you and in those who are following you.
- Confidence decides who will trust you.
- Confidence destroys fear.
- Confidence creates self-worth.
- Confidence decides your access to another.

Week Thirty - Nine

OVERCOMING THE POWER OF SHAME

"THIS DAY I HAVE ROLLED AWAY YOUR APPROACH... SHAME OR GUILT..." JOSHUA 5: 9

"**M**an is the only creature that BLUSHES:" "Man is the only creature that cries over its mistakes..." If the Animal Kingdom operated like man, they would not survive... they would starve. When an animal fails in conquering to feed, they don't sit around and cry about their failure. No, they get up and find something they can conquer so that they can eat.

I believe that the most overlooked emotional wound is **SHAME!** This feeling of shame hinders us from taking our position as God's handiwork on the earth. Every time we take a step towards our rightful place with God, the enemy reminds us of our mistakes and failures. What happens next is how the enemy controls us. We begin to flood our emotions with shame. Many of us equate shame with being UNLOVEABLE, WORTHLESS, UNREDEEMABLE, OR CUT OFF... Many of us are ashamed of being ashamed! In some cases the feelings of shame and guilt can lead to SUICIDE.

Shame strikes the deepest into the heart of man! Shame can be felt as inner torment, a sickness of the soul. Some have described shame as being humiliated, or feeling naked. When Adam, in the book of Genesis, had disobeyed God, he immediately had awareness that He was naked. God asked Adam, "Why do think you're naked, or who told you that you were naked?" What I believe Adam was feeling wasn't his nudity, but rather the shame of being exposed. What entered mankind was horrible! This sense of shame and guilt had never been experienced. Below is a list of what, I believe, entered that day into the human race.

THE OFFSPRING OF SHAME:

Alienation, helplessness, powerlessness, defenselessness, weakness, insecurity, rejection, rebuffed, stupid, dumped, uncertainty, intimidation, , defeatism, ineffectiveness, inferiority, flawed, exposed, unworthiness, hurt, peculiarity, different, bizarre, and oddity.

Shame, is often experienced as the inner, critical voice that judges whatever we do, as wrong, inferior, or worthless.

Shame lives in the area of this **inner critical voice** that was birthed in us and is repeating what was said to us by those who were over us, such as our *parents.... a relative... a teacher and even our peers.* We may have been told that we were NAUGHTY, SELFISH, UGLY, STUPID, etc.

We may have been DISLIKED BY PEERS AT SCHOOL, EMBARRASSED BY TEACHERS, TREATED WITH DISAPPROVAL BY

OUR PARENTS. Sometimes, those around us, or above us, are never satisfied with our efforts, or performance, they are critical no matter what. Unfortunately, these criticisms **become internalized**, so that it becomes our OWN INNER CRITICAL voice that is calling out the shaming messages, such as: *"You idiot, why did you do that?"* *"Can't you do anything right" or "You should be ashamed of yourself" etc*.

One source of shame is associated with the expression of *certain emotions*. In many families, as well as, in many cultures, expressions of such feelings as, **anger, fear, sadness, or vulnerability, may be met with shaming reproaches, such as** "PULL YOURSELF TOGETHER" "DON'T BE A BABY" "STOP CRYING, OR I'LL GIVE YOU SOMETHING TO CRY ABOUT" OR "YOU DON'T HAVE ANYTHING TO BE AFRAID OF".

Pride is also a feeling that is often met with shameful condemnations, such as "WHO DO YOU THINK YOU ARE MR. BIG SHOT" OR "YOU'RE GETTING TOO BIG FOR YOUR BRITCHES." Too often these shaming admonitions are internalized,.

Clearly, these shaming inner voices can do considerable damage to our self-esteem. These self-criticisms, that we are stupid, selfish, a show-off, etc., become, in varying degrees, how we see ourselves.

For some of us, the inner critical judge is continuously providing a negative evaluation of what we are doing moment-by-moment. As mentioned before, the inner critic may make it impossible for one to do anything right, telling you that, "**You are too aggressive**" or "**Not aggressive enough**" "**You're too selfish**" or "**You let people walk all over you**".

Week Forty

NINE STEPS TO A MIRACLE HARVEST OF PLENTY

NINE STEPS TO A MIRACLE HARVEST OF PLENTY:

I believe this is the year of completion; God is going to complete the struggles and pressures we have endured in the past years. This is the year of plenty. There is about to be a harvest released upon the body of Christ that is going to anger the enemy.

Proverbs 13:22 says that the wealth of the wicked was stored up for the righteous. I have been having my congregation say out loud:

"WEALTH OF THE WICKED, COME TO ME NOW!"

Before we can move into the nine steps of receiving a miracle harvest, we first, have to come into agreement that God wants us to be prosperous. Prosperity is the most feared and attacked word in the church. Many religious believers will "turn off" those who state that they believe in the prosperity message; you may be called fanatical, or humanistic.

Those who do not understand prosperity make statements such as: "All they care about is money" or, "They're focused on money and not ministry."

Nothing could be further from the truth. What do you think it takes to keep ministries operational? What does it take to keep websites up and running... to broadcast on television, to reach millions with the gospel? What do you think it costs to travel, to keep the power on, mortgage, phone; to put gas in the bus?

It all requires money.

I'll tell you why I think the prosperity message takes a hit. The word "prosperity" only appears in the Bible seventeen times and most of those are in a negative concept. However, the word "peace" appears four-hundred and twenty-nine times; ninety percent of the translated meaning of the word "peace" means prosperity!

Translators of the Bible used the English word "peace" for the Hebrew and Greek word "prosperity." In my opinion, they should have left the word prosperity. This one, mistranslated word, has caused wars in the body of Christ.

The Bible declares we are soldiers in the army of God *(Ephesians 6.)* We are to stand; we are to fight the good fight of faith *(1 Timothy 6:12)*. How can we have peace and also be warriors? Warriors are not needed in times of peace. God was not talking about peace...He was talking about prosperity. Truth understands that you will never experience peace until you are prosperous.

Let me take just one of the **429** references and show you a very well known verse.

"Stand therefore, having your loins girt about with truth, and having on the breastplate of righteousness; and your feet shod with the preparation of **the gospel of peace**.*"* Ephesians 6:14

Strong's # NT: 1515 eirene (i-ray'-nay); probably from a primary verb **eiro** (to join); **peace** (literally or figuratively); by implication, **prosperity**: KJV - one, peace, quietness, rest, + set at one again.

Did you read it for yourself? Does the translated word in the origin imply prosperity? Of course it does. We are to, shod are feet with the gospel of prosperity... Not the gospel of peace, because peace is prosperity! If you have been one of those who try to fight the prosperity message, maybe you should stop for a moment and think. Where did your reason to disagree come from? Was it from the Lord and through study, or was it from your spiritual, religious, denominational teaching?

I am convinced that I have people in my church that do not want to grow... learn... or be mentored; however, they want to argue and fight the very message that God sent Jesus to die for. Think for a moment... What did Jesus die for? To pay a debt you couldn't pay. Why? You can never be called prosperous if you have debt you cannot pay.

The one debt that you could never pay was the debt of sin. We use to sing an old song in the church... *"He paid a debt He did not owe, I owed a debt I could not pay, and I needed someone to wash my sins away. Now I sing a brand new song amazing grace. Christ Jesus paid a debt that I could never pay."*

II Kings 4:1-7, tells a story of a widow whose husband had died and left her in debt. The creditors were coming to take her two sons and sell them into slavery to pay the debt. This widow was in a hard place. Have you ever been afraid to answer the phone in fear of being hounded by the creditors? This widow lived in a time where she couldn't go to the court system to file bankruptcy. If you couldn't pay, you were arrested.

STEP ONE: *KNOW WHERE TO GO WHEN YOU DON'T KNOW WHAT TO DO.*

The first place this woman runs to is the Man of God. Elisha was the head of all the prophets. Many times, when we are in this kind of predicament, we tend to run to everything we think can get us out. Why do we always try natural abilities first? This widow had good sense to run to someone who could give her a word from God.

STEP TWO: INVENTORY WHAT YOU ALREADY HAVE.

The Man of God asks her two major questions.
1. *"What shall I do for thee?"*
2. *"Tell me, what hast thou in the house?"* II Kings 4:2

The first question implies that he doesn't have the means to help her; that even if he collected an offering from the other prophets, there still wouldn't be enough to meet her need. Most of the prophets had been drained by the attacks of Jezebel during this time. All the prophets at this time were in financial struggle.

The second question digs out the means in which he could work her faith to unlock God's hand of mercy. **"What do you have?"** Take an inventory. There is something you already have that will produce everything else you will ever need.

STAY WITH ME!

God is not going to bring you anything until you have something you can **release for Him to multiply**. He is a God of warfare, not welfare... Many of us have been led to believe that

God is going to bless us solely because we got saved... I don't care how much you earn, how big your house is, or how nice your car is, if you expect God to move, then He's going to expect you to move too. Whether you're in prosperity, or lack, you must do something. "Not equal giving, but equal sacrifice." God will get involved in what you are willing to release, sow, or use for your increase.

YOU DO WHAT YOU CAN! GOD WILL DO WHAT YOU CAN'T!

STEP THREE: YOUR PERCEPTION COULD BE COSTING YOU DEARLY

"Thine handmaid hath not any thing in the house, save a pot of oil." II Kings 4:2

Perception isn't truth, perception is *your* truth. If your perception is distorted, then your truth will be distorted. She perceived she had nothing for God to use. What a lie from hell! That's how Satan works... he wants to blind us from seeing the miracle in small things. Perception is the power of your own reality. All she had was a pot of oil.

I can see the prophet's mind whirling. He had discovered the one thing that God could use to create everything she needed. She had to look past her perception and see what God saw. *She was in the right place for a miracle harvest of plenty!* Would she take another look? How about you, will you take another look?

STEP FOUR: LITTLE THINGS MATTER

Her perception was that she had nothing but a little oil. She assumed that her pot of oil was too small to create anything. Little hinges swing open huge doors. Small keys unlock huge vaults containing millions of dollars. Again, a small key can crank up machinery that can move mountains. *"For who hath despised the day of small things?"* Zechariah 4:10

Many will never achieve greatness because they fail to see the power of small things. *"Well done, thou good and faithful servant: thou hast been faithful over a few things, I will make thee ruler over many things: enter thou into the joy of thy lord."* Matthew 25:21

STEP FIVE: FAITH ISN'T FAITH UNTIL YOU DO SOMETHING WITH WHAT YOU HAVE.

Faith requires action. She had to work her faith; she had to believe beyond the crisis. Faith is the ability to see your future success while facing your present problem. What did the prophet do? The prophet instructed her to go and borrow more pots from her neighbors… he instructed her to go and get in more debt. *"Go, borrow thee vessels abroad of all thy neighbours, even empty vessels; borrow not a few."* 2 Kings 4:3

I'm convinced that many of us couldn't be lead by the Bible leaders. We would never allow a person to speak to us with such authority. We have too much of our pride and opinion that blocks the pure revelation of the man of God. Have you noticed in the Bible that most of the time God used a man of God speak to His people?

STEP SIX: SMALL INSTRUCTIONS CREATE HUGE MIRACLES

When Jesus wanted to produce a great miracle, He always gave small instructions. Go wash at the pool of Siloam…and a blind man was healed. Launch out into deeper waters and cast your nets… fill water pots with water and the best wine was produced. The reason you may not be experiencing a miracle harvest of plenty could be that you are unwilling to follow a simple, godly instruction. Great miracles do not require great instructions. Great miracles require obeyed instructions. The prophet instructs her to go and borrow more pots.

An ignored instruction can be very costly. Jonah disobeyed God's instruction to go to Nineveh. Instead, he boarded a ship to escape his last instruction and while Jonah on board a storm appeared. This storm wasn't scheduled for anyone but Jonah; however, everyone else on the ship had to suffer the ill weather and destruction of the storm because of Jonah's disobedience. What happens next blows my mind! The people on the ship, assuming they were the reason for the crisis, start throwing all their goods over the side, hoping that this act of sacrifice would appease the gods. Jonah came forward and informed them that the storm wasn't because of anything they had done; it was the result of his disobedience. He instructed them to throw him off the ship and the storm would cease. Understand, it's not what's in your life, but who's in your life that could be costing you. Small instructions create huge miracles and ignored instructions can create deadly curses.

STEP SEVEN: SHUT THE DOOR...

Shutting the door represents a dual purpose. When you shut yourself in, you have to also, shut something out. Why did the prophet tell her to go and shut in, then start pouring? He knew that to shut in with God would shut out distractions, the voices that may have tried to talk her out of her act of obedience. Do you desire a miracle harvest of plenty? Go ahead and plan for it... expect it! Shut yourself in with God. Get an encounter with God that is bigger than the crisis you are facing.

STEP EIGHT: MOVE BEYOND THE MIRACLE...

This step is very crucial. The miracle happened when the

little jar of oil never ran out to fill all the jars she had borrowed. Many of us would have never left the room. We would have been so enamored with the miracle; we probably would have stayed in the room and built a church. This would have cost her dearly. The process to being debt-free wasn't in the pouring of the oil, but in selling it.

STEP NINE: THERE WILL ALWAYS BE MORE THAN ENOUGH...

"Then she came and told the man of God. And he said , Go, sell the oil, and pay thy debt, and live thou and thy children of the rest." II Kings 4:7

I love the last verse of this story. The widow's only request to the prophet was to help her with her debt; but when God gets involved, He always looks beyond the request, to the miracle harvest of plenty. She sells the oil to pay her debt... then she and her sons have a lifetime income of selling oil. The prophet tells her to go and live on the rest.

I'm expecting this to be the year for your miracle harvest of plenty!

Week Forty - One

TWENTY – FIVE YEARS
TWENTY – FIVE KEYS

I hope this week you will take the time to learn from my mistakes. The list of keys, or quotes I have provided, I trust, will help you quicker than they helped me. Some of them, I had to learn on the back-end of a mistake.

The problem with life is, that we get old too soon and wise too late.

THINGS I'VE LEARNED

"There is no fruit which is not bitter before it is ripe."

"To advance to the next season you must be willing to sacrifice

what you "are" to become what you need to be."

Better to be sent... than to be called for... When you are sent by God, you are better equipped to complete the task than for someone to call for you.

Don't get so focused on the process, that you worship the furnace and forget the fire.

The highest order in life is not doing, but becoming...

There is a difference between getting something and receiving something. You didn't get Jesus you received Him. You don't get a gift, you receive a gift.

The clearer the instructions... the less confusion people will walk in.

The difference between a burden and a blessing is possession.

Don't allow the accolades of people to outweigh the principles of God... It is very easy to overlook God's principles when all you can hear is the praise of those around you.

Compromise is the road to deception...

Competence is more memorable than kindness.

This key came to me while I was in Jacksonville, Florida. I was assisting Dr. Murdock at one of his conferences. He was going through a difficult time with the bridgework he just had done. He had changed his dentist and his present dentist was chosen because of his kindness. Sitting in the restroom applying some temporary cement, the man of God looked at me and said, "Competence is more memorable than kindness."

Passion is more memorable that performance.

The wrapping is as important as the gift…

Those who haven't suffered your pain will not understand your purpose.

Favor is the reward for godly obedience.

Productivity is the proof of favor.

Those who haven't paid your price will never understand your praise…

Learn to weed out and move swiftly away from the non-favored.

You will never be like Jesus, until there's a Judas who betrays you and a Peter who denies you.

Success is not attached to talent, but what you do with that talent. Ability without pursuit is useless. The talent of a person is his ability to do it better than the normal… the heart of the talented is his ability to continue to play when he is losing.

Promotion comes to those who become overqualified. Why should promotion come if you haven't overqualified in your present season?

Proof you're connected is your reaction to correction. When your mentor stops correcting you, your future no longer matters to him.

Your present has no meaning without your past. Stop complaining about your past. Your past survival qualifies you for your future endeavors.

Success, healing, and happiness have no power when your

present is always watching your past.

Hope cannot exist if there is no dream for your future.

Reality is flawed... Illusions have no flaws.

"Life is what you do, while you're waiting to die..." Donald Trump

God never promised a harvest by where you sow, but by what you sow. I have since reevaluated this one. I believe the power of your harvest is also attached to the soil you sow into. We must make sure the soil is worthy of the seed we plan on sowing. If you have recently sown a seed and later found out that the soil wasn't what you were led to believe, remember, God still honors the seed.

"Those who know what they're doing always have a job, those who know why, are always their boss." Mike Murdock

Never leave your ministry... discern your ministry.

"Anything that begins in anger will most assuredly end in shame."

Let me share just a few mistakes I've made along the way. I hope they will help you this week.

MISTAKES I'VE LEARNED ALONG THE WAY...

Responding to the needs of people, instead of God's voice... This one cost me dearly. Needy people are never satisfied. Needy people will drain the resource that's in you and leave you for the next sucker. Jesus never made the needy His focus. He always spent more time with those who wanted to learn... who wanted to be trained. He led those He could influence. This is not to say, that you should shut out the needy, it's just to caution you not to make them your focus.

Few Ideas are God ideas... I've wasted a lot of money, time and resources on this mistake. Few ideas are God ideas. First and foremost, God ideas will always produce increase. Not every good thought is the voice of God telling you to do something. Labor to recognize God's voice and when He speaks, it will usually sound like you.

Friendliness is not integrity. Just because a person is kind and nice, doesn't mean that they're honest and truthful. Character, is what you are when no one is looking. Friendliness is what you do to be noticed.

MENTORSHIP MOMENTS:

Wisdom is a shortcut to success...

My future is being decided by who I choose to believe...

It's very dangerous when your mentor stops correcting you... your future no longer matters to them...

Stop advising those who don't value your judgment.

Week Forty -Two

FOUR "C's" THAT STOP PROGRESS

The deadliest place to be in your walk with God this week will be a place of complaining. I understand these four "C's" better than most because I lived in them for so long. The first 'C' is complaining.

STOP COMPLAINING:

God hates complaining:

Complaining is an utterance of pain, displeasure, or an annoyance.

"That our oxen may be strong to labour; that there be no breaking in, nor going out; that there be no complaining in our streets. Happy is that people, that is in such a case: yea, happy is that people, whose God is the LORD." Psalm 144:14-15

Notice, happy is the person who *does not* complain. When the children of Israel complained, God usually acted in judgment over them. God held the window of opportunity open all night, but the children of Israel wouldn't stop complaining long enough to see the victory that was set before them. By morning, God decided to shut the window and send them on a forty year journey for their disobedient attitude of complaining.

People that pay for things never complain. It's the guy you give something to that you can't please. ~Will Rogers

In trying to get our own way, we should remember that kisses are sweeter than whine. ~Author Unknown

STOP COMPARING YOURSELF WITH OTHERS:

The next "C" is, *comparing.* No one will ever succeed trying to compare themselves to those around them because their only focus is on the strengths of others. As a result, they are never satisfied with what God created in them. You are a one-of-a-kind masterpiece, fashioned by the hand of God. You have a purpose that no one can fulfill but you. Focus on being the best "you" you can be and celebrate God's creation of you.

"And the second is like it: 'Love your neighbor as yourself."
Mathew 22:39 NIV

People who are always comparing themselves with others have a poor value system. They dislike what they are, and who they are, and they're always in search of what someone else is, or what someone else is doing. Jesus was very clear on this. You are unable to love your neighbor, if you are unable to love yourself. To compare, is when you are looking at something and you consider its worth over yours. This never works!

Trust the Lord. Learn to value you! You are God's handiwork. You are fearfully and wonderfully made (Psalm 139: 14)

DISCOVER YOUR DIFFERENCE THIS WEEK: You will only be celebrated for them. God has made you unique... there is no one else like you. You have an assignment that belongs to no one else but you. So, why not take the time to discover why you are here.

STOP COMPETING WITH THOSE AROUND YOU.

Competition is healthy in some cases, but in others, it can be deadly and create anger and frustration. Competition creates rivalry. Competition causes people to dislike each other. During competition, someone has to lose. God never intended us to compete with each other over success, our homes, our jobs, our finances, and for love. You may have heard someone say, "It's not good to try to keep up with the Jones's." Now, I have no idea why the "Jones's" are so popular, but I can tell you this; if you want to become financially broke, start trying to keep up with them. I once heard someone say, "Let the Jones's keep up with you, its much cheaper."

Love and competition do not mix. It is impossible to love something you are competing with. Competing causes opposition. Love creates unity. Love wants to give... Love is self-sacrificing. Competition strives to win... Competition desires to take, not give. God can't use those who are always competing in the church.

Say this right now, *"This is the last day I will wish I had someone else's equipment."*

STOP COMPROMISING WITH WHAT IS RIGHT:

Compromise is killing the church. To compromise, is to settle. When we compromise, we are adjusting to opposing principles. Now, how is God going to bless someone who makes it a practice of giving up their principles?

Compromising Christians are those who live halfway between right and wrong. These halfway-Christians are too far out to be in, and too far in to be out, there just stuck in the middle. The Bible calls them, *Lukewarm.*

"So then, because you are lukewarm, and neither cold nor hot, I will vomit you out of My mouth..." Revelation 3:16 NKJV

God can't stand a lukewarm Christian. He so hates them that, He says He's going to spew, or vomit them out of His mouth. It's better to be either hot, or cold. Now, at first glance, you would think that this is hard.

If you're hot, then you are where you need to be, and at least if you're cold, you will be in search of what can warm you, but to be lukewarm, means you have become comfortable. Comfortable people have a hard time with the word "change". When you've stopped changing, you're finished!

Make this the week that you deal with the four **"C's."** Ask the Holy Spirit to help you stop **complaining**, stop **competing**, stop **comparing** and stop **compromising**.

Week Forty -Three

MAINTAINING JOY IN TROUBLED TIMES

The church is full of good singing... Good preaching... Great talent and wonderful musicians... We have advanced to the place where we can produce movies... own television stations... build great buildings... the world has noticed our advancement.

Let me ask you this one question... *with all of this increase, where has our joy gone?*

With the increase of what is required from us to survive and live, we have allowed our daily needs to rob of us what God intended for our lives. Living the life of JOY!

"But let all those that put their trust in thee rejoice: let them ever shout for joy, because thou defendest them: let them also that love thy name be joyful in thee.   For thou, LORD, wilt bless the righteous; with favour wilt thou compass him as with a shield."
Psalm 5:11-12

The quickest way to embarrass the enemy is when we walk in joy!

When the enemy has flung everything within his arsenal, hurts... wounds... betrayal... financial problems... etc. When the smoke clears and he sees you still standing, and not just standing, but standing with joy on your face, it's that joy that will embarrass him. Joy will embarrass the enemy!

The proof of God's presence is joy.
"Thou wilt shew me the path of life: in thy presence is fullness of joy; at thy right hand there are pleasures for evermore." Psalm 16:11

When we decide to walk in God's presence, a sense of power and might will proceed in us. We will begin to walk in real power and joy and in that joy, there are pleasures. We will experience more from our daily life. More than a sense of accomplishment, or worldly gain, we are experiencing real peace. Isn't that what we are really in need of today? (Peace)

Failure is the quickest way to lose your joy;

We have all failed in one way or another. Excepting God and trying to walk a godly life doesn't exempt us from pain... defeat... lack... or mistakes. *A godly life is a vulnerable life, not a protected life!* Once you understand this, you will begin to do what is necessary to build protection around your personal environment. Atmosphere matters to God. You can be saved from hell, but have such a bad atmosphere around you that, God doesn't desire to be around you. The issue isn't that we are comfortable with God, but is God comfortable with us!

When you decide to walk in a godly lifestyle, you now become the target of those who are inferior to your change. What has caused you to be different? You now have an atmosphere of joy. Let me warn you… this is not a place of protection; it is a place of warfare. To maintain your joy, which I call peace, prepare for war!

The first way to maintain your joy is to understand how to protect your atmosphere.

What things have you allowed around you that are destroying your focus? What music do you pump into your spirit? What are you listening to? Who are you listening to that is affecting your faith? Discern who Satan has placed around you that have gotten your attention. There is the doorway to your defeat. Protect your environment!

KEYS ABOUT ATMOSPHERE:

1. Atmosphere decides your climate. Climate influences your emotions and feelings.
2. Atmosphere can be changed by the smallest things.
3. Nobody else can create your atmosphere for you.
4. Order creates a peaceful atmosphere.
5. Atmosphere decides your performance potential. You will never perform to your best potential until you recognize that atmosphere matters.
6. What you are viewing daily will decide what kind of atmosphere you are living in.
7. Colors can create moods and affect your atmosphere.
8. Your atmosphere can often determine your productivity.
9. What you see and hear is affecting the decisions you are making.

Your attitude can affect your joy.

Take an inventory daily of your attitude. Your attitude can greatly affect what is happening around you. A bad attitude pollutes the air and destroys the power of faith. If you are a person who always sees the negative side of things, you are more than likely, a very unhappy person. Why? Because your bad attitude blocks the sunshine of love, hope and expectation of change and increase. Your bad attitude creates a gloomy cloud that hovers over you and steals the presence of God from you, creating an atmosphere void of all joy.

There is a scriptural cure for this. Psalm 27:6 says; *"And now shall mine head be lifted up above mine enemies round about me: therefore will I offer in **his tabernacle sacrifices of joy; I will sing**, yea, I will sing praises unto the LORD."*

Offer up a tabernacle sacrifice of joy. This kind of lifestyle takes effort. You have to make a decision to walk in a sacrifice of praise. Sing always to the Lord for He is good! Let me give you another verse we quote all the time in the church.

"For his anger endureth but a moment; in his favour is life: weeping may endure for a night, but joy cometh in the morning." Psalm 30:5

Everybody will have bad days no matter how saved they are. When you find yourself in a weeping moment of stress and pain, remember, they can only last for a night, for joy comes in the morning! Why? It's in the night while you sleep that you are disengaging from yesterday's failures and reconnecting into today's victory.

FIVE FACTS ABOUT THE VALLEY OF MISTAKES:

1. Failure is inevitable; the question is will you keep making the same mistakes over and over?
   Look at Philippians 3:12, 14
2. Mistakes remind us that we are not God and we are in need of Him.
3. Failure helps most of us to find God. It causes us to see

things through His eyes. God loves to build upon our ashes... God uses are weakness to extract His Strength. (Psalm 103: 13, 14)

4. Repeated mistakes warn us that we are stuck in a rut...
5. Failure is always the first step to success...

FAILURE IS NEVER FINAL!

HOW TO GET THROUGH FAILURE:

1. Acknowledge God's Presence;

It's during the times when you least feel His presence, when it seems that God has moved and didn't leave a forwarding address, that God does His best work in us.

2. Adopt an Attitude of Gratitude:

Only a thankful heart can praise Him. Find the good that is already in your life. Start to develop a heart of thankfulness. The ungodly are always unthankful...

3. Ask God for His Guidance;

a. Jeremiah 33 "Call on me and I will answer you....." (Read it)
b. Galations 5:16 – 18

4. Align Your Perspective to God's:

Your perception is your truth, but not necessarily *the truth*. Make sure you have God's views and not your own. Your perceptions can be costing you dearly. I don't want to live my entire life, and face God and hear Him say; "Son, your whole life was a lie. Son, you believed a lie and called it truth."

Prosperity can create seasons of joy:

*"Let them shout for **joy**, and be glad, that favour my righteous cause: yea, let them say continually, Let the LORD be magnified, which hath pleasure in the prosperity of his servant."* Psalm 35:27

Patience can create seasons of joy:

"The LORD is good unto them that wait for him, to the soul that seeketh him." Lamentations 3:25

We need to learn to wait on God. He is good to them who wait. Isaiah 40: says that God gives us strength when we wait on Him. Not just strength, but "renewed strength". A power will overwhelm us and cause us to mount up on wings of joy, and peace. We will fly like the eagle. Our ability to wait on God creates a power season of joy. This joy will take us to heights that will be above what is trying to defeat us… what is trying to discourage us. God has called us to fly like eagles, not live like buzzards, sitting around eating what has already died. God hasn't called us to eat what others have planted. God has called us to live a life of joy and happiness!

Joy is the power of the Lord revealed in our lives.

Stop allowing the things around you to steal your joy. God has called us to walk in His joy. This is only going to take place when we stop living life for the things around us, and start living life to please God.

If you like this message, order the CD series "GOD WILL TURN YOU SET BACKS INTO COME BACKS."

Week Forty - Four

ARE YOU HUNGRY OR THIRSTY?

Could you be in need of a drink? Maybe, what you really need is, not another sermon, or preaching tape to listen to, maybe, what you need is, for God to rain water over your life. When you lack water, you lack the very substance that makes all the other gifts work. Water, in the Bible, always represents the Spirit. Water is the life-source of everything on the earth. Water is what the Holy Spirit is in our life. He is the life-source to all that God has for us. Without Him, we are dry and thirsty.

The Holy Spirit is the most misunderstood part of the gospel. Is He only in us if we speak in tongues? No, and if not, then we must deal with the question, has speaking in tongues left the church? The answer again, is no. But can we function without speaking in tongues? Yes. Do we need the power of tongues today? Once again, yes! Let me encourage you to seek the all of the gifts, not just one. While you're seeking the gift, seek the giver of the gift and not the gift itself. Go ahead, take a drink. Try for once, to allow the Holy Spirit to reveal the water, and when He does, don't close up the window of your faith. Let the rain of heaven fall! The Bible speaks of rain over 102 times. Rain is necessary!

I was reading a magazine the other day and an article caught my attention. The article was about dehydration. It stated that, most Americans are not getting enough water and one of the reasons was, because there are so many substitutes, such as soda, tea, juice, coffee, etc. These drinks can create a false sense of hydration.

Hungry or Thirsty:

Because there is a lack of water, many people who are hungry, may actually just be thirsty. The article went on to say that, many are overweight because they are trying to satisfy with food, what they think is hunger, when in actuality; it is their body craving water. The next time you have hunger pains, drink a glass of water, if the hunger pains leave, then you weren't hungry, but thirsty.

While I was reading, the Holy Spirit began to deal with me. I began to question; could it be, that the church is thirsty? Could it be that, we are satisfied with food, when what we really need is for God to open the windows of heaven and give us a spiritual drink?

Symptoms of dehydration:

Thirst, dry mouth, sunken eyes, weak plus, lack of suppleness in the skin, cold hands and feet, confusion, lethargy, difficulty in being aroused... This sounds like a lot of churches to me. What we need isn't another sermon. What we need is an outpouring! We need for God to send the rain!

Didn't Paul warn us about the last days? Didn't Paul mentor Timothy that there would be these kinds of thirsty believers, who would have the form, but deny the water. They would look like those who had a holy life. They would even appear to be righteous, but in the end, they would deny the power, the water, and the Spirit. I think he did.

"... always learning but never able to acknowledge the truth. 8 Just as Jannes and Jambres opposed Moses, so also these men oppose the truth-men of depraved minds, who, as far as the faith is concerned, are rejected. 9 But they will not get very far because, as in the case of those men, their folly will be clear to everyone." II Timothy 3:7-9 NIV

The proof you are spiritually hydrated is the power to endure. Endurance is the proof that you have not just been eating, but you have also been drinking. Water is the key source of the power. I once explained it this way. Too much word and no spirit and you'll dry up; too

Those Who Endure Have the Right to Be Heard

much spirit and no word, and you'll blow up. But if you have a balance of the Word and Spirit, you'll grow up!

I make this statement because drinking is not enough. Eating is not enough. For the physical body to be healthy, it needs a balance of the right foods, with the proper amount of water and exercise if you want to stay strong and mobile. Of course, there are more intense things we must do, but this is not a book about health, well, not physical health. This is a book about ending your drought. It is a book that is designed to open the window and encourage you to seek for rain.

The balance is necessary. First, you must understand that you can live longer without food than you can without water. Water is more vital than food. The Spirit, first, and foremost, enables the food (Word) to find a place where it will cause you to change and grow. More than once, the Word of God uses an important phrase about hearing. *"He that hath an ear, let him hear what the Spirit saith unto the churches;"* Revelation 2:7

Someone, once said, that man can live seven days without water, and thirty days without food... So, we must conclude, that water is three times more important than food. Yet, food is what we spend most of our time stuffing in our mouths. The same is true in the spiritual realm. Why do we eat more and drink less? Because food satisfies more, it satisfies our taste buds, our emotions are affected by certain foods. We use food as our comforter when we should be using the Holy Spirit. Food is a stimulus, and water really has no taste. Water is just for substance. Water is the life source of the body. Water is neutral! It doesn't affect the emotions, it affects the body. I believe the same is true in the supernatural. The preaching of the Word is good, but it also feeds the emotions. The Word in itself can be tasty. Someone, who is animated, can preach and have you crying, laughing and shouting all in one message. It is through preaching that the ears of people are stimulated. But if we are not careful, the water of the Word will be ignored. The water has no taste. It has no *pizzazz*, it only has the power to fill and nourish. It's very easy to believe we're always hungry, when in fact; we are in desperate need of water.

This reminds me of a story of a woman who was living in a time when being of a mixed race was really looked down upon. This woman lived over two thousand years ago in a city called, Sychar, in a place called, Samaria. This story takes place in John chapter 4, where a certain woman had been living in the worst of the worst of times. First of all, she was half Jew and half Philistine.

I believe this woman was crying out to God everyday. Knowing that she was forbidden to go to the local church, she had to cry out in her pain. Maybe she was asking God if half of her was enough to fix her. She knew that one half of her bloodline has always been at war with God, but what about the other half? Could that be enough? The side that was of the race of God, would God give this side rain? Well, the answer is, absolutely! While Jesus was on a journey somewhere else; he made an effort to go by the way of Samaria. While he was waiting at Jacobs well, she came to Him. He was sitting, watching her climb the mountainside to get to the well where she had dipped in for most of her life. But today was different. Today, was the day someone would dip in the well to give her a drink of real, supernatural water. The rain is about to fall in her life.

"Jesus answered and said unto her, If thou knewest the gift of God, and who it is that saith to thee, Give me to drink; thou wouldest have asked of him, and he would have given thee living water..." John 4:10

This woman had to accept that her life could be different. In the water of the Spirit, there is enough of God to stop the drought. This water is supplied by the rain of heaven. This water will allow her to never thirst again. This was living water! This was the place where sin abounds, but grace abounds much more. Without this kind of rain, there would never be any real change and she was about to change!

Do you want to know how she was fixed? Think about this, she obviously had a relationship problem. She was married five times and now she was living with the sixth man. The wounds of her past and the imprinting of racial issues have been very costly to her. Jesus is not the one who is going to fix her, well, not by Himself. She has to get involved if she wants this water. First, she has to be willing to dip in her well and fetch Him some water. If you don't want to dip in the well of your pain, and wounds one more time, God is not going to open His never-ending supply of water to you. When you dip in this well, you can not do what you have done for so long; that is, drink from it. No, you have to be willing to give this drink to Jesus. When you can give it to Him, He will make the exchange and give you what is in His well. When she let go, God let go, and rain fell from heaven; enough rain that she would never run out and enough rain, that you and I will never run out. All we have to do is give God what is in our well.

EIGHT AREAS THAT CAN STOP THE RAIN:

1. *Your racial issues*
2. *Wrong relationships*
3. *Unforgiveness*
4. *Bitterness*
5. *Unwillingness to face your past*
6. *Your religion*
7. *Your condition (wounds)*
8. *Your inability to recognize Jesus*

Week Forty - Five

OVERCOMING THE POWER OF SIN

SIN SHALL NOT HAVE DOMINION!

"Likewise you also, reckon yourselves to be dead indeed to sin, but alive to God in Christ Jesus our Lord. Therefore do not let sin reign in your mortal body, that you should obey it in its lusts. And do not present your members as instruments of unrighteousness to sin, but present yourselves to God as being alive from the dead, and your members as instruments of righteousness to God. For sin shall not have dominion over you, for you are not under law but under grace." Romans 6:11-14 NKJV

Sin has been defined as many things...In the 1800's, we had the inquisitions and the investigations. Everybody in church leadership went on witch-hunts. You were considered to be possessed if you didn't act according to the opinion of others. People were arrested when they acted strange, or

CHANGE YOUR HABITS... CHANGE YOUR LIFESTYLE

"out-of-the-norm". They were put on trial in what were called, "witch trials". Usually when someone was taken to trial they were convicted of "being of the devil". This conviction usually meant a penalty of death by drowning, or being burned. When these so-called "demon possessed people" were tortured, it was believed that it would drive out the evil spirit; thus, freeing the witch, or warlock from the influence of it. How convenient it was to accuse someone and then do away with them without ever having to take the time necessary to help them. What a messed up system that was! This is what I call, "looking for demons under every bush". I don't believe that there are demons under *every* bush, but I do believe there are demons under *some* bushes.

Religion was very stringent on what you could, and could not do. In the early part of the twentieth century, they used phrases like: "Walk holy"... "Live holy"... "Don't do anything to mess up your walk with the Lord". The church became *rule oriented*. Man began to equate holiness with the way you dressed, talked, ate, drank and acted.

The leaders of the church set up *watchers* to tell on those who didn't live up to the rule. They made sure that every Christian was miserable. I am not bashing where we came from. However, I am concerned that we have taken our walk with the Lord a lot less serious than those who have gone before us. I wish that we could come to some middle-ground on the understanding of what "walking with the Lord" really means.

Let me interject, it was never God's plan for us to separate, or to walk away from something...a bad habit, wrong attitudes, substance abuse, spirit of anger, etc. No one can really walk away from their desires, or problems, without some understanding of what they are walking into. Try to change your focus instead of trying to change your walk and your lifestyle of sin. What you focus on you will eventually become. What has your attention is mastering you. Trying to walk away from actions that you have been doing for years is almost impossible. **Change your focus and your habits and you will change your lifestyle.**

LAW OF DISPLACEMENT:

You don't focus on the darkness if you want to expel the darkness in a room. You don't have to work up your faith, or confess that the darkness is gone. What you do is flip the light switch on, and the entry of the light forces the darkness to exit.
Quit crying about it... and start doing things differently today! We need to seek to grow closer to the Lord. God had to prepare the children of Israel for a new way of living when He brought them out of Egypt. Allowing them the time to go through the wilderness did this. God had to change them from a "welfare" mentality, to a "warfare" mentality in the desert. God had to take out an entire generation to get His plan fulfilled. God changed their focus from what they were to what they were becoming. It was a new mentality of possessing and not being possessed; not a spirit of moving from, but moving to something greater than where they had been. The difference between a burden and a blessing is possession!

When I was a youth pastor, young people would come to me and say, "Pastor Jerry, I have this sin, how can I come to God with all these problems?" My reply was, **"Come as you are.** God will take you as messed up and dirty as you can come. When you start entering into God's presence... He will begin to clean you up. **Just come!"**

- Come as you are...
  - Come addicted...
    - Come hurting...
      - Come angry...

Reminds me of the old Hymn; *"There's room at the cross for you, though millions have come there's still room for one..."*

SIN IS NOT YOUR PROBLEM

Whatever you have done, or are doing, just make sure that you don't ignore God's leading. Take that step of change and come to Jesus. We need to renew our passion for the name of Jesus. It seems that we have become enamored with so many teachings; Faith, Prosperity, Healing, Confession, Motivation, Favor... What we need to focus on is, the Name of Jesus. Jesus said if we would lift Him higher, He would draw all men unto Him. Maybe our churches aren't growing the way we would like them too... Could it be our focus, is on everything, but the right thing? God said build up My name; I'll build your church. If the Lord doesn't build the house, the laborers labor in vain.

God's complete plan is for you to be free from the control of sin and to have a clean life... I believe we can live such a life. We are not to separate from Him, but to separate to Him! We are not to separate from sin...but separate unto Jesus! The closer you get to Him, the less you will sin. Sin is an acronym for **S**TOP **I**T **N**OW! Stop running away from your weakness and start running to the Lord!

What is sin? It is **DISOBEDIENCE**! That's it. No great thesis, or phrase, just one word. Sin, is disobedience to an instruction from God. It doesn't matter whether that instruction comes from the Bible, or from your parents, or from your spiritual leaders. If the Word of God can back the instruction, and you disobey, you have at that moment, sinned. Sin exists from the gutter... to the pulpit. The Bible declares that sin is "lawlessness."

"Whoever commits sin also commits lawlessness, and sin is lawlessness..." 1 *John 3:4 NKJV*

The Greek word for "lawlessness" is *"anomia,"* which

means, "the condition of being without law, because of ignorance of it, or because of violating it." Lawlessness means not submitting to the laws, or authority of God. Sin is the consequence of something much deeper in us. What causes me to want to break God's laws and submit to something else?

The author R.C. Sproul says: **"YOU CAN HAVE NO SOUND THEOLOGY, WITHOUT SOUND DEMONOLGY."**

How does sin become the result of what causes consequences in my life? What causes us to sin? The truth is that we sin, because something in us drives us to sin. I don't believe that people by the majority, live to sin. I do not, in any way believe, that people want to sin, or that they study and strive to be sinners. There is a greater force in us that drives us to sin. Sin is not the cause, but the consequence of the cause. Sin is not the problem. Sin has no power over us and by the scripture we just read... "Sin shall not have dominion over you". Sin shall not rule us. We should be ruling sin!

SIN IS DISOBEDIENCE.

Anything you do, contrary to what God has said to do, is sin. Sin is the cobweb, not the spider, or the problem. Sin, is the consequences of something greater and deeper in all of us. There is something much greater in us that causes us to sin. However, I'm not ready to dive into the discovery of the spider just yet. We need to gain some greater revelation on some basic rules before we can move into and discover what the spider is.

"Sin shall not have dominion over you." **Sin shall not rule our domain.**

What is dominion? **TO RULE IN YOUR DOMAIN!**

In **Romans 6**, the word "dominion" in the Greek is "Kurios", which means supremacy, or supreme in authority (i.e. controller.) Sin shall not have supremacy over you... sin shall not control you. It's not that we aren't going to sin; it's that we are not controlled by sin. We must first stop sin's control over us in order to be free from the bondage of sin. Do we have to keep on doing what we know is wrong? Does sin have that much dominion over us? If so, then this would make **Romans 6:14** wrong. I believe that once we discover what's causing us to sin we will stop building our lives around the consequences of sin.

To rule is to dominate an area in which we are ruling. To dominate is to rule, or control by superior power. We must understand that we have been given power to rule and to dominate this earth. I know that the popular persuasion is that when the first Adam in Genesis fell, he gave up the earth to Satan, and now Satan owns the right to dominate, rule and control.

"**WORSHIP CREATES FOCUS**"

I do not give into this persuasion because God never gave Adam the earth. He only gave him dominion to rule while He was not present.

"The earth is the Lord's, and the fullness thereof; the world, and they that dwell therein. For he hath founded it upon the seas, and established it upon the floods." Psalm 24:1-2

"The earth is the Lord's and the fullness thereof, the world, and they that dwell therein". God never relinquished the earth, nor did He ever give control of the earth to Adam. If God never gave Adam control, then we must also assume that Satan never gained control either. Adam had nothing to release, or to let go of. He wasn't the owner, he was just being allowed to rule while God was not present. The power of withstanding from the curse of sin is first, to let go of complete control.

When we understand that God is: All-powerful,

(omnipotent) all-knowing (omniscient) and ever-present at all times… (Omnipresent) …we will let go of control. Adam ruled until God showed up, then Adam would bow. He would worship God and in his worship, he would give God His proper place; **DOMINION.** Adam would maintain his focus. His focus wasn't to rule over Eden, but to worship Almighty God. Real worship is unrehearsed. Real worship comes from the heart and not from the song leader, or church choir. Worship prepares us for God's blessings. It changes our focus from ourselves, to God. Worship, is the ability to bow and promote whom we are really connected to. Worship, allows us the avenue to find comfort and access into God's presence.

You see, the truth, is that Eden wasn't created for Adam, it was created for God. Eden was a place carved out of the earth where God could dwell in communion with whomever He desired to allow into His garden. Adam wasn't the ruler of Eden. Adam was only allowed to control the earth while God was absent from Eden. Eden's atmosphere was conducive for God to enter it. It was God's place, and as long as man walked according to His instructions, he could walk freely in God's atmosphere. Have you created an atmosphere where God wants to dwell?

The ability for Adam to let God have dominion over him, gave him the ability to have dominion. The spirit of humility is, to give God His proper place, which places you in proper order and position. The proper position is dominion and not a position to be dominated by anything, or anyone, but God. We become arrogant and self-centered when we lack the humility to relinquish our kingdom for God's Kingdom. When we allow God His proper place, He begins to allow us ours.

THE GREAT QUESTION:

Lucifer saw man and his relationship with God, and he became jealous. After all, Lucifer was the best God could do without making him God. Lucifer, which means "light bearer," was the light carrier of God. He brought all of heaven to worship and then carried that worship to God.

One day, Lucifer began to look at himself. He saw his flawlessness, and he began to receive worship unto himself. Lucifer was found holding back worship for himself when he brought God His rightful worship. This is one of the reasons the tithe needs to be paid. Don't be caught holding back what rightfully belongs to God. He became self-conscious instead of God-conscious. Lucifer was defeated the very moment he conceived the thought of keeping what was rightfully God's.

I'm not of those who believe that there was a long drawn out war in Heaven between Lucifer and his angels and God and His angels. I believe, the moment God became displeased with Lucifer, Lucifer was forbidden to experience God's atmosphere, and was sentenced for eternity, to stay out of the presence of God. Satan, is now, cast down to the earth where he can dwell without the power to be forgiven. We must have a clear understanding that Lucifer must have ruled on the earth before Adam was ever created.

Eden wasn't created for Adam. Eden wasn't created for Lucifer. Eden was created for God to have a place where He could come to earth and walk, or dwell among His creation. Lucifer was in Eden before man was... possibly before he even fell. *"Thou hast been in Eden the garden of God..."* **Ezekiel 28:13**

In Luke Chapter 10, Jesus tells us that all authority was given unto Him... That He saw Satan cast out of heaven like a lighting bolt... Some time before **Genesis Chapter 1:-2,** all this took place. Dr. Kelly Varner says, *"Once upon a time when there was no time, in a place called nowhere on the back side of nothing there was a meeting. Present in that meeting was God the Father, God the Son, God the Holy Spirit and you. Lucifer had already been cast out, the Lamb had already been slain, resurrected and was sitting at the right hand of the Father."* We know that in **Ephesians,** Paul states that, we were made before the foundations of the earth: *"Just as He chose us in Him before the foundation of the world, that we should be holy and without blame before Him in love..."* Ephesians 1:4 NKJV

Think for a moment. This pristine, picture-perfect God, whose only obsession is order; *order is the accurate arrangement of things,* has a world sitting out in space... full of darkness, void and nothing on the earth is complete. Just floating there, sticking out like a sore thumb. How long had the earth been in that state? Only God knows how long. No one in Heaven would dare to mention, or talk about it. (*Genesis Chapter 1*)

Imagine the surprise of all the angels and demons when all of a sudden, the Spirit of the Lord starts hovering over the face of the deep. Notice, that the Spirit is always in the place where the Lord is about to speak up. The Holy Spirit knows the thoughts of God. Now, God speaks over the earth and declares "LET THERE BE..."and there it was! We should always speak after the Spirit moves. Don't just stop and wait for someone to preach when praise and worship is over in your services. Take some time to speak. Speak over your life! Speak over your children! Speak over your finances and let the atmosphere be permeated with your faith!

God decided to move from where He was to being present on the earth, after He had spoken all things into existence. Here is where I get "goose bumps." God begins to play with dirt until he finds an image He likes. Everything on the earth, and in the earth, God spoke and there it was. He didn't need to do anything, but speak. *Hebrews 11* declares that, we know that the Word of God framed the worlds. God said, "Let there be light!" and there was light, and it stayed where it was told to stay and hasn't moved. When God speaks... His word is everlasting to everlasting. Then, it's time for God to do something that is definitely contrary to what God has ever done to this point. God decides not to speak man into existence, but to come down and touch man. God forms man by moving dirt around until He is satisfied with an image. Then, He exhales so that man can inhale. God breathes into man, and man becomes a living being. When God exhaled, the Spirit of God entered into man. Blood began to flow through man's flesh. The Word declares that life is in the blood.

All of the habitants of the earth and Heaven stood in amazement. Lucifer, Gabriel and Michael are all watching as God steps out of character. This God, the Creator of all things, reaches out and touches dirt? Then, He does something that absolutely takes all of Heavens breath away. God begins to reach for a gift to give this creature, called man. God is going to crown man, and what does He crown him with... not a crown of gold, not a crown of silver, nor pearls, or emeralds. He looks all over and begins to ponder, "What is the best I have to put on this flawed creature?" God crowns him with His **GLORY!**

SIN SHALL NOT HAVE DOMINION

What do you think Heaven must have been thinking, when all during this time, they have all, secretly longed for that touch? Man was the only thing that ever received God's touch. The truth for today is that, man has been in need of a touch from God since that day. Giving man a piece of God's Glory must have sent Lucifer into a frenzy. After all, wasn't that what Lucifer was longing for, to grab hold of the Glory of God? Now, here's God giving this precious gift, not to a perfect creature like Lucifer, Michael, or Gabriel, but to this flawed, imperfect, creature called, MAN!

Lucifer must have stared for days at this creature, trying to figure out what it was about Adam that drove God to come everyday and walk with him and talk with him. Lucifer is about to go mad... He can't figure this one out...what is this flawed and weak creature that has God's attention like no other creature? So, here comes *Psalm 8*, the question that must have put Heaven in absolute silence while all of the angelic hosts are waiting for God's answer. **What is a MAN...?**

"What is man that you are mindful of him, and the son of man that you visit him? For you have made him a little lower than the angels, and you have crowned him with glory and honor." Psalm 8:4-5 NKJV

"LORD, what is man, that you take knowledge of him? Or the son of man, that you are mindful of him?" Psalm 144:3 NKJV

After all this drama, God speaks to man and blesses Adam, and then gives him complete and total power, or dominion over God's affairs. *"And God blessed them, and God said unto them, Be fruitful, and multiply, and replenish the earth, and subdue it: and have dominion over the fish of the sea, and over the fowl of the air, and over every living thing that moved upon the earth."* Genesis 1:28

The Hebrew word for "dominion" is: "Radah" (raw-daw'); *a primitive root; to tread down, i.e. subjugate; specifically, to crumble off.*
Copyright (c) 1994, Biblesoft and International Bible Translators, Inc.)

Sin shall not have rule, or dominion over you. Sin shall not tread you down. Sin shall not cause you to crumble, or be broken off the whole anymore. God has made provision for the penalty of sin. However, we are still not where we need to be. We must keep searching for the cause; to discover the cause, can fix the consequences. Life is made up of cause and effect. Sir Isaac Newton's law applies here as well.

Week Forty - Six

PRINCIPLES OF GODLY STEWARDSHIP

STEWARDSHIP EQUALS RULERSHIP!

The great debate in the Kingdom of God, is does God expect us to have plenty? Should I give, and if I give, should I expect something for it?

I have never understood why people become so incensed over giving. Then it dawned on me. It's not the giving that angers people. People give all the time. We give to all kinds of charities and schools, etc. The spirit of anger comes in, when we attach to the equation, the attitude that when we give, we should expect God to give it back to us.

GIVE IT, AND IT WILL BE GIVEN BACK:

What is it? Well, first, let's look at the scripture I am making reference to.

*"Give and **it will be given to you**: good measure, pressed down, shaken together, and running over will be put into your bosom. For with the same measure that you use, it will be measured back to you."* Luke 6:38 NKJV

Give and it will be given back to you. **What is it?** It is anything you have sown, or given. Now, I didn't write this verse. The word *"give"* appears 881 times in the King James. Give and it will be given back to you... The King James says "....would men give back to you." NIV says it will be poured into your lap. What God is trying to say, is that if you give, expect something for it. This is not unscriptural, this is God's wishes. God has always attached results to our actions, good, or bad.

GODLY PRINCIPLES:

PRINCIPLE OF THE SEED

Everything started, or starts with a seed. *A seed is a tiny beginning to a huge future.* Small seeds can move huge mountains. If you don't like your harvest, change your seed. The greatest power in the universe is the power of a sown seed. I've seen grass crack cement. Think of how powerful a seed is and how strong the life in that seed is, when a blade of grass can find a way to crack cement.

Some have a problem with the word *seed*. They prefer to call it an "offering". Well, I want to call it what God called His giving. *"And I will put enmity between thee and the woman, and between thy <u>seed</u> and her <u>seed</u>; it shall bruise thy head, and thou shalt bruise his heel." Genesis 3:15.* God called His giving a *seed*. God sowed His Son (a seed) and reaped a harvest. Us!

Whatever you do, don't fight one of the greatest teachings in the Bible besides the cross, and that is, if we sow, we can expect a harvest for it. There will never be a day that you have nothing to sow. You are a warehouse of seeds. Kindness is a seed. Time is a seed... Love is a seed... of course, money is seed.

PRINCIPLE OF EXCHANGE

You have something someone else needs and wants. Income is increased by the law of exchange. The law of exchange is, when you release something you have, to create something you want. You go to a restaurant and you exchange money for food... to the mall, you exchange money for clothes. You desire money; you exchange your time for it. I believe you get the picture.

PRINCIPLE OF THE MIND

Your mind is your world. The world you live in is not your world. The world you live in is the world you *think* you live in. *"For as he thinketh in his heart, so is he..."* **Proverbs 23:7** Reality is not what you live in; reality, is what you *think* you live in.

The greatest soil in your life is your mind. We will spend hundreds of dollars on our stomach, our clothes, etc., and spend very little on our minds. Yet, what is happening around us is the result of what is happening in us. What the eyes see, and the ears hear, usually, the mind believes. The mind creates the world you live in. The mind dictates your emotions. A thought creates an emotion, and an emotion creates an action. If your emotions are wrong, then your reactions to them will usually be wrong.

Your mind is a garden. Let me ask you a question. What seeds are you allowing to be planted in your garden? There's not a greater seed sower than our enemy Satan. He's sowing everything he can into destroying your mind and when your mind goes, so goes your future. *Keep thy heart with all diligence; for out of it are the issues of life.* **(Proverbs 4:23)** Guard your heart… This is your mind. Protect it at all cost. WHY? Out of it, you set up your boundaries. All emotional wounds live and breathe in the mind; our past hurts and pains that we won't allow the mind to forget and heal. Holding on to what was, is costing us what is. God has a future for all of us; yet, our minds can't release where we came from, to create where we are going.

The mind has two major abilities, memories and imagination. Memories are the thought process of where we have already been. Imagination is the thought process of where we are going. The only way to enter your future while you are still in your present is with your imagination. This is why Paul instructs us to cast down false imaginations. (2 Cor 10) Why? False imaginations create false futures… vain futures.

PRINCIPLE OF FAITHFULNESS

Faithfulness is a lifestyle. What is faithfulness? It's being committed to the truth even if it costs you everything. I believe faithfulness is the ability to stay connected even when you are feeling the strain of your connection. Showing up even when you are tired and stressed out. Faithfulness is doing what's right while everyone else is doing wrong. Faithfulness is a decision, not a feeling.

How many days do you miss work in a year? Do you steal from your employer? The usual answers to these questions are, "Not much." and "No." Yet, God is more important than your job. Let's be as committed to God's laws and desires, as much as we are to ours. Let this be the week you change and increase your faithfulness.

PRINCIPLE OF ORDER

Order is the accurate arrangement of the things. Order, is placing something where it belongs, not where you leave it. Order is one of God's obsessions. God is a planner. God is the God of order. Is your life in order? Do you have life insurance? Do you have a will? Do you have a savings plan? Have you set goals on how this year will be different from last year? Do you have a get-out-of-debt plan?

Take the time to get your life in order. Without a growth plan you will surely be planning your demise.

Take this week and work some of these principles into your life. This is by no means an exhausted list, but this list will help you get on the right track.

Week Forty - Seven

DEMOLISHING SATANIC STRONGHOLDS

"For though we live in the world, we do not wage war as the world does. The weapons we fight with are not the weapons of the world. On the contrary, they have divine power to demolish strongholds. We demolish arguments and every pretension that sets itself up against the knowledge of God, and we take captive every thought to make it obedient to Christ. And we will be ready to punish every act of disobedience, once your obedience is complete." 2 Corinthian 10:3-6 NIV

IF YOU GIVE SATAN A FOOTHOLD HE WILL TURN IT INTO A STRONGHOLD. Dr. Jerry Grillo

God has provided for us a victorious lifestyle. We are to be a person that overcomes the enemy. I've heard people say,

"We're in it to win it." Not so, we are not "in it to win it" because through Jesus, we have already won it! We are winners because He (Jesus) won it on the cross!

The will of God is revealed through the Word of God. His instructions to us are as follows.

- We are not to war in the flesh.
- The weapons of our warfare are mighty.
- Our weapons are empowered by God.
- Our weapons are to pull down strongholds.
- Our weapons cast down vain imaginations.
- Our weapons pull down high things which are against God.
- Our weapons bring our thoughts into captivity to Christ.
- Our weapons are held in readiness to avenge all disobedience when our obedience is fulfilled.
- The word of God in our hearts and on our lips sets the captive free. (Isaiah 61)

WE HAVE THE RIGHT TO USE THE BLOOD:

"And they overcame him by the blood of the Lamb, and by the word of their testimony; and they loved not their lives unto the death." Revelation 12:11

The blood of Jesus is your greatest weapon. The blood makes a statement without saying a word. When you show up to the battlefield and you have been blood-washed and blood-stained by your connection to Christ, your presence alone speaks. The blood speaks for you.

Through the blood, we have redemption and forgiveness. (Ephesians 1:7) Thus, the enemy can't hold your past over your head.

~223~

Through the blood, we are justified (Romans 5:9) Satan has no legal hold on you to accuse you guilty.

Through the blood, you are sanctified. (Hebrew 13:12)

Through the blood, we are being cleansed. (1 John 1:7) The dirt of sin and wrong living, through Jesus, has been washed clean.

Through the blood, we are healed. (1 Peter 2:24) Sickness can no longer be a stronghold on us.

Through the blood, we are made temples of God. (1 Corinthians 6:19-20)

The old hymn rings true. "There is power, power, wonder, working power in the blood." "What can wash away our sins, nothing, but the blood of Jesus…"

AREAS WHERE STONGHOLDS LIVE:

1. **The mind.** Now, we don't have to spend a lot of time here. I dealt with the mind in the last chapter. Just let me add this. The mind was to be dominated by the Spirit of God and not by the sensuous desire of the flesh. You are made up of body, soul, or mind, spirit, will and emotions. When man fell, his mind fell.
2. **The church** (religion) if we're not careful, we will try to validate our denomination and void out our relationship with God. We were to dominate in our dominion, not spend our time defending our denominations. In my opinion, religion is one of the strongest strongholds Satan has. We will ignore the truth of God's Word because someone told us different. We will stay in a dead church and die in the pew, and believe the whole time that we're okay and alive in Christ. What a stronghold!

3. **The environment around you.** Assess the environment when you enter a room. Atmosphere matters to God. What's going on around you may affect what's happening to you, and in you. Thoughts are not limited to a certain person, or place. Thoughts could be flying in the room through the atmosphere looking for fertile ground to house in. Remember, Satan controls the airwaves. (Ephesians 6) He is the prince of the power of the air. Discern what spirits are in the room. If you don't control your environment, someone else will.

4. **Your past.** Some hurtful experience behind us can still be affecting what's going on around us. Something we have failed to deal with could possibly have caused bitterness and unforgiveness in our hearts. It may have been a parent. Maybe a teacher... Could be a church hurt... a spouse betrayal... Whatever it is, if you haven't dealt with it and placed it in the love of God, it's a place where Satan could be mounting His stronghold attack on you.

Past regrets...past hurts... past feelings are strong walls of defense for the enemy. Satan loves for us to keep looking back. What happened to us in our past is never the issue. It is how we are handling it in our present. God cannot heal what we are unwilling to face. Let go of what was, grab hold of what you are about to be and do. Let people off the hook that have hurt you. They are no longer the issue. Someone once said to me, "I wish I never had a past." This is wrong thinking. **Without your past, your present would have no meaning and your future would have no purpose. Your mess is going to become your message!**

5. **Your perceptions.** You could be walking in what you think is truth, yet, the whole time, you are deceived. Perception is your truth, but it's not necessarily *the truth*

We all have had to fight strongholds. It's not a shame to have one, but it is a shame to keep them. I once read a book about strongholds and it listed general categories. Let me give you this list.

Fixations, compulsions, obsessions, addictions, fears, anxieties, delusions, undiagnosed illnesses, curses, eating disorders, sleeping disorders, stress-related disorders, prejudice systems, religion, greed, anger, pride, bitterness, jealousy, lust, perversion, resentment, spite, laziness, negativity, false accusations, intimidation, guilt, lying, confusion, and suspicion. There is so much more, but this is enough to give you the victory

FACTS ABOUT STRONGHOLDS:

❖ All of us have them.
❖ None of us are as free as we can be.
❖ None of us are as free as we want to be.
❖ None of us are as free as Jesus died to make us.

DEFINING STRONGHOLDS:

❖ An area where wrong reigns.
❖ An area of secrets that has not been exposed. Satan does his best work in the dark places.
❖ A thought pattern that is contrary to the Word of God.
❖ Anything in us that keeps us from changing into what God has created. The world says; you are who you are; God says you are who I created you to be.
❖ A thought pattern that seems to be truth, yet it is based on what man says, and not what God says.
❖ A place where the enemy's ways seem more credible than God's ways.
❖ A wounded heart where bitterness lives and anger rules.
❖ Reactions that have caused disobedience.

I command this week, that the strongholds you are facing are being destroyed by God's Word. God tears down walls, but men take cities. God tears down the walls that are destroying you, but you have to take back what the enemy has stolen.

Week Forty - Eight

GOD LONGS TO HEAR THE RIGHT VOICE

A hard word from God is better than no word from God.

God is searching the earth and He's longing to hear a certain cry coming from the earth.

The voice of Repentance:

The first time the Son of God speaks to a group of people He uses the word *repent*.

"From that time Jesus began to preach, and to say, Repent: for the kingdom of heaven is at hand." Matthew4:17

Think about this for a moment. The first real message that God's Son preaches, is the message **"Repent for the Kingdom of heaven is at hand,"** not, "Well done" not, "You are blessed" not even a, "Hello" and "Boy, do we miss you in heaven". The first message is *repent*.

First of all, you must have a clearer picture of these two themes: *repentance* and *the Kingdom of heaven*. This will give us a clear understanding to what Jesus was speaking about.

If you believe that the phrase **"Kingdom of heaven"** is pertaining to just a certain place; a place where we are all going when we die, then you will probably miss the real meaning behind the word **repent**. The Kingdom of heaven is not just a place where we are going when we die, but rather, the phrase is speaking of a mind-set. There's a different mind-set in those who connect to this Kingdom, than those who are living in the earth.

Repent means to turn around... To think about what you are doing. The Greek word means, to make a 180 degree turn. Stop going one direction and start going another. For this to happen, you must make a decision. First, you must decide that you are going the wrong way and second, that you have the wrong way of thinking since you are heading down the incorrect path.

Repentance doesn't mean to just stop doing... Repentance means, to change the way you are thinking and then you will change the way you do things. First, and foremost, God is longing to hear the cry of repentance in our churches and on the earth.

The voice of Intercession:

The secret of praying, is praying in secret. I call prayer the ability to approach the thin place where heaven and earth meet. That's where a human can talk to God and begin to see things God's way. **Intercession** is when we begin to seek heaven for man's sins. Intercession is not our time with the Lord, but time spent on someone else's behalf. If there has ever been a time to pray for others it's today. When people start calling out to God for the sins of others and have a repentant heart for the wickedness in their city, God will hear from heaven and show His mercy and grace.

Think of those around you who are suffering or sick, and speak to God on their behalf. What you make happen for others, God will make happen for you. (Ephesians 6:8)

The voice of Wisdom:

Wisdom is simply, knowing what to do next. Wisdom is **applied** understanding. God is longing for us to start making better decisions and it takes wisdom to make them. There are circumstances and situations coming that will demand that we have God's mind-set to get through them. Wisdom, is acting in God's mind-set and not your own. Wisdom, is when we are sensitive to the instructions of the will God no matter what.

The voice of Expectation:

God will give you everything you are expecting Him to give you. When you take expectation out of the earth, you rob God of the ability to be pleased. Wake up everyday and expect God to do the miraculous. Sow your seeds and expect God to increase them. Pray for healing and expect God to heal you. Expectation is a magnet. Expectation means that I believe. Do you believe that something good is about to happen? I do! Do you believe that this is your day for God to show you incredible favor? I do!

Do you believe that God wants you blessed, wealthy and healed? I do! God's going to give it to you any way you want it. So, if you don't believe, then guess what, He's not going to do it. He will respond either way.

The voice of the Seed:

Every seed sown cries out to God for increase. Seeds have

a voice. When God is looking over your life, He wants to hear the seed you've sown speaking out. What is your seed saying...? They're saying, **"Increase me!"**

Your seed is God's last memory of you. When Cornelius, in Acts 10, was going to church, the Jews didn't allow him to come into the building. So, Cornelius would send his money in his place. God sends Peter to Him and tells him to bless Cornelius.

*"And when he looked on him, he was afraid, and said, what is it, Lord? And he said unto him, Thy prayers and thine **alms (seed) are come up for a memorial before God.**"* Acts 10:4

God's memory of you was your last offering.

The voice of Love and Forgiveness:

We've got to stop all this fighting and hurt in the church. Why is it, when people leave one church for another, they always seem to dislike the people they left. Come on! We've got to stop all this anger! Walk in love. Love is the greatest weapon we have against the enemy.

Love is the most powerful force on the earth. The Bible says, "Love never fails….. Love bears all things….." Love will cause you to holdup under all kinds of pressure. The proof that Jesus is in you, is that you love one another. We have got to walk in love if we plan on walking in victory.

Week Forty - Nine

ABIDING IN THE POWER OF THE SPIRIT

"In Him you also trusted, after you heard the word of truth, the gospel of your salvation; in whom also, having believed, you were sealed with the Holy Spirit of promise who is the guarantee of our inheritance until the redemption of the purchased possession, to the praise of His glory." Ephesians 1:13-14 NKJV

First, and foremost, we must understand that people build people. People help people win and heal through their crisis. God uses people to mend people through the Holy Spirit, which is the Spirit of God.

For us to walk in the power of the Spirit, we must understand the Godhead. I believe in the triune Godhead. I believe, there is God the Father, God the Son and God the Holy Spirit, they're different, yet, one in assignment and agreement. I like what Pastor Benny Hinn preached years ago. **God is the Commander.** Everywhere you see the Father, you see Him saying LET THERE BE...

Jesus is the doer. He is fulfilling and working to completion everything the Father wishes. He is the doer of the word. When God needed to redeem man, Jesus came and made it possible through obedience.

The Holy Spirit is the source, the power in which they operate. He is the manifestation of what God wishes and Jesus does. He is the person who walks beside us to empower us to fulfill what Jesus died for and all three work together to make this a reality.

Let me give you an example. If I say, "Let there be light" that's the command, the voice of the Father. Someone walks across the room and turns the light switch on. That person is working, or walking out my wish, my command. They are the doer of the Word, or Jesus. But the light, when it is illuminated and the darkness is expelled from the room by the power of electricity, that is the Holy Spirit.

The Holy Spirit is the key to walking in the power of God. He's the One that brings what Jesus is doing to life. He's the life sustaining, power-giving, source on the earth. He's the One walking beside you, guiding you... convicting you... encouraging you... He is Jesus in us.

The Power of the Spirit reveals things to us.

"But God hath revealed them unto us by his Spirit: for the Spirit searcheth all things, yea, the deep things of God. For what man knoweth the things of a man, save the spirit of man which is in him? even so the things of God knoweth no man, but the Spirit of God. Now we have received, not the spirit of the world, but the

spirit which is of God; that we might know the things that are freely given to us of God. Which things also we speak, not in the words which man's wisdom teacheth, but which the Holy Ghost teacheth; comparing spiritual things with spiritual. But the natural man receiveth not the things of the Spirit of God: for they are foolishness unto him: neither can he know them, because they are spiritually discerned." 1 Corinthains 2:10-14

The Power of the Spirit moves things away from us...

The things that you will not allow God to move in you could cost you what God wants to reveal to you. I've heard it called, *The Law of Displacement.* When something enters your life, something has to exit your life.

The entry of one, forces the exodus of the other. That's THE LAW OF DISPLACEMENT. In the church, we have been conditioned, and imprinted to pray things out. But maybe, the more accurate way to look at this is, to pray for more of something else to enter. More of God... more goodness... more love... more money... and the entry of one will force the exodus of the other.

When the Spirit moves in, He will begin to move out what doesn't belong. Allow the Spirit to do His job. I promise you, you will not be disappointed in the end. Now, just a note, you may not like what He moves out at first, but it will be for your best in the end.

Week Fifty

SEVEN BATTLE KEYS FOR DEFEATING THE GIANT

"And he stood and cried unto the armies of Israel, and said unto them, why are ye come out to set your battle in array? Am not I a Philistine, and ye servants to Saul? choose you a man for you, and let him come down to me. If he be able to fight with me, and to kill me, then will we be your servants: but if I prevail against him, and kill him, then shall ye be our servants, and serve us. And the Philistine said, I defy the armies of Israel this day; give me a man, that we may fight together. When Saul and all Israel heard those words of the Philistine, they were dismayed, and greatly afraid." 1 Samuel 17:8-11

You can't win wars by evacuation, you win wars by confrontation. A person who flees from warfare is not a warrior, but a refugee. Let me say this, refugees will never win a battle, nor will they ever conquer the enemy. A refugee is a person who flees from a battle, or religious persecution. I made the declaration in my church, The Favor Center; that the church was never supposed to be a refugee camp. The church was designed to be a house that trains soldiers to fight. We are in a conflict! The giant is screaming at us! The enemy is laughing in our faces. He is declaring that there is no God in the church!

IN MY CHURCH THE REFUGEE CAMP IS CLOSED.

I'm not advocating that we shouldn't help those in need, or even those who aren't willing to fight. But, I am saying, that we need to stop spending all of our time helping those who aren't going to eventually stand up and fight.

THE WISDOM CAMP FOR WARRIORS IS NOW OPEN AND READY FOR BUSINESS.

BATTLE PLANS:

1. DON'T DESPISE BROKEN PLACES:

When God is ready to release us, He will find something that will break us. Our broken places are where the anointing comes from. Broken people who survive their brokenness become burden breakers themselves. Those who are burden breakers are God's anointed. Those broken places were necessary for you to discover your destiny. Thank God you survived what others died in. Never despise your pain.

2. BECOME A WORSHIPPING WARRIOR:

Praise is easy. Praise, is thanking God for what He has already done. I praise Him for my car, my health, the food on my table, etc. Praise is external. The only qualification for praise is breath. Let everything that has breath praise the Lord. (Psalm 150:6) Praise is temporal. Everybody can praise God. The sinner can praise. The tree's can praise. Worship, on the other hand, is totally different. Worship is internal. Worship comes from the heart. Worship, says I don't care about what happens to me externally, I will worship no matter what. Worship, is the persuasion that God is able even if He hasn't brought what you wanted to pass. Worship comes from the internal source of faith. Praise is talking to God about what you can see; Worship speaks to God about what you can't see. Before David became a warrior, he was a worshipper. His worship developed the warrior within him.

3. WARRIORS ASK THE RIGHT QUESTIONS.

First question, **what do I get if I fight?** David wasn't about to fight the giant until he first knew what He was going to get for it.

- **Never Go To War Where There Are No Spoils!**
- **Never fight an enemy that can't increase you when you win.**
- **Reward is the reason we should enter the fight.**

How did David know that Goliath was his assignment? The spoils were equivalent to the dignity of His anointing. David was anointed to be King by Samuel. When David heard what the rewards were, he knew he was anointed for this battle.

Second question, **who is this uncircumcised Philistine?** In David's mind, the issue was about covenant. The issue was promise. This enemy facing him, no matter how big he appeared, was not in a covenant relation with David's God. David knew that, **covenant will sustain you!** When God gives us an impossible promise, He does so, to sustain us in impossible times. David had been given a promise. No one else knew what He was anointed to be, but David knew. When God puts something in you, your life cannot be finished until all has been fulfilled.

Being confident of this very thing that He who has begun a good work in you will complete... (Phil 1:6 NKJV)

4. YOUR WILLINGNESS TO STAND ALWAYS FORCES THE COWARDS TO BE REVEALED.

Don't let this upset you. When you decide to change, you will force those who aren't with you to surface. David's older brother came out from behind the rock to confront David and his decision to fight. Eliab wouldn't come out from behind the rock to fight with Goliath, yet, he would risk being noticed to confront David.

Eliab looked like a king, and walked like a king. But when you're the top coward hiding with all the other cowards, you're not exposed until someone is willing to stand, where they were willing to hide. Eliab says "David I know you... You are here because of your pride." Isn't it funny, how those who are never around you, always seem to know you when you decide to fight the enemy they where were hiding from? No one knew that Eliab was a coward until someone decided to be different. Expect someone to oppose you when you stand to fight. Expect it to be someone you thought you could trust.

5. PROTECT YOURSELF FROM WORDS OF DISCOURAGEMENT.

Eliab said to David, "You can't fight this giant. You've never fought in any war, or battle." David must have been thinking. "It's obvious you haven't read the local newspaper." While I was out tending daddy's flocks and worshipping God, a lion came out and I slew it. One night, a bear came out and I killed it. While I was worshipping God, I was also practicing my skills as a warrior. David was ready.

6. WILDERNESS IS NECESSARY FOR MATURITY.

While David was in obscurity, God was developing him for his destiny. David worshipped God in private and God allowed him to excel in public. God had been preparing David for Goliath. David was faithful in the little things and God was preparing him to be ruler over big things. Remember, the faithful are always anointed, but the anointed, are not always faithful. What I mean is, there are those who come in and look like Eliab and walk like Eliab, but when the enemy comes in, they will hide. They appear to have the gifts and talents, yet they are never faithful. Don't let anyone discourage you from your destiny.

7. *I**F YOU DESPISE WHAT** G**OD IS DOING NOW IN YOUR LIFE YOU WILL NEVER BE PREPARED FOR YOUR FUTURE.***

Let me make this so simple you will need someone to help you to misunderstand it. WAX ON! WAX OFF! Remember the karate kid? He didn't understand the assignment in his present. He thought he was just waxing cars, but his mentor was building muscles for his future enemy. The same is true with God. You may think God's abusing you. You may feel He's abandoned you. You could even feel He's forgotten about you. Just keep waxing. God is preparing you for your future.

When you fight, be comfortable being you. Don't try to wear other people's accomplishments. Make your own way. God has your life in His hand. Trust Him! Trust God today.

Declare that today is the poorest you will ever be the rest of your life! The rest of your life is the best of your life!

Week Fifty - One

THERE'S A POWER SHIFT

THERE'S A POWER SHIFT... GET READY TO BE ANOINTED!

For anyone to be truly anointed, they must first, understand the price of the oil.

It cost the olive everything to become the oil!

In the Old Testament, we see olive oil as the type and point of contact for the description of the anointing. When they placed the oil on the forehead, or right ear and so forth, they were professing that you were anointed. The word anointed means, to be smeared on, or rubbed down. This oil was to be poured on you and as it flowed over you, it would signify that God's covering was flowing over your life. The anointing is more than just good preaching, singing, or teaching. The anointing will allow you to break the yoke off of someone's life. So many are hurting, and carrying a heavy yoke of fear, financial lack, wounds, and pain. There are so many people who are looking for someone who is anointed to break that yoke.

There are four major ingredients that make up the anointing oil. Myrrh, Calamus, Cassia, and Cinnamon… Now I know there is one more, but let's deal with four first. Now four, is a transitional number, 40 is a powerful number. Four is transitional and zero is an eternal number. If you add zero to any number you increase it ten times. Add zero to one and you have ten. Add zero to ten (10) and you have one hundred (100). Add zero to one hundred and you have one thousand (1000). **Do you see the power of zero?**

Four, is also a significant number. Four is the transitional number between three (3) which is resurrection and five (5) which stands for grace, or favor. Something is being changed in you between resurrection and favor. In the tabernacle, there were four poles to get through in the outer court, there were five poles to enter through to the Holy Place and there were four poles of pure gold to enter the Most Holy Place (Holy of Holies). Four, five, four! In Genesis, God hung the sun on the fourth day and on the four thousandth year God hung the Son, called Jesus. There were four men in the furnace. There were four lepers who stopped a famine. There are four gospels to enter the New Testament and Lazarus was dead for four days, so the number four must have great meaning.

The first and most powerful ingredient is Myrrh… Myrrh is bitter, and represents the wilderness of loneliness and drought. To be anointed you have to first survive the Myrrh. With Myrrh, there was a fifth ingredient, Frankincense. Frankincense is the counter part of Myrrh. Jesus is the fifth ingredient to be anointed. He is the Frankincense. He's the One person who can bring calmness and sweetness to a bitter life of Myrrh. Both are the main ingredients in producing the anointing oil. Now, of course there are the other ingredients, but for the sake of time, I will have to expound on them later.

To be truly anointed, you must submit to the pulverizing of the mixture in the bowl of change. This means that you must first, lose your own identity, and in the process of being pulverized, you begin to digest and receive the mixture of the other elements. The first season of the anointing is frustration, pain, stress, and attacks. **Expect ridiculous attacks when you are about to show off your anointing.**

The anointing will force a power shift in your life...

The truly anointed will force a power shift in the church... If the anointing does not drive something out, it is not genuine. It is called the "**law of displacement**." Instead of trying to overcome something, or to force something to leave, first, try to allow something to enter. The entry of one thing will force the exit of the other. The entry of light forces the darkness to exit. The entry of the anointing will force the exit of what is burdening you. Remember, there is always a counterfeit to the genuine. There is human energy that is mistaken most Sundays in churches for the presence of God. We have become masters of the fake and exuberant. Cheerleading is the menu of the day in most churches. But cheerleaders don't win games, coaching does.

Two kings were picked to rule Israel....one was picked by the people; the other was picked by God.... FAVOR KEY: **WHATEVER PROMOTES YOU HAS TO SUSTAIN YOU.** Do me a favor, go look up the word "sustain". There is more to that word than you can imagine.

When Samuel went to anoint Saul who was chosen by the people, he used a bowl. When Samuel went to anoint David, who was chosen by God, he used a ram's horn. Why the difference in utensils? The bowl was man-made and Saul was chosen by man. The Ram's horn was not made by man, it was made by the Creator, God and David was chosen by God. Whatever anoints you, whatever promotes you, has to be able to hold you, and sustain you. If self promotes you, then self has to sustain you when trouble and crisis come. Believe me, they will come. In those times of hurt and trial, you better have more than a self-promoting or man-made anointing. You better have been anointed and appointed by God.

When you are anointed, you don't have to possess the best to be the best, you just have to be anointed. David was anointed and chosen by God. Let me give you some keys about those God is about to use to do great exploits.

ASSIGNMENT REVEALS YOUR DESTINY FOR GREATNESS!

Take any assignment you can get... it might be the assignment that takes you to your promotion. David is asked to take milk and cheese to the battle field.

Always be ready to defend God's honor. David was insulted by the enemy's words against God. One of the proofs that you have really been anointed will be your willingness to defend and maintain the honor of God at all cost.

Expect others to resent your willingness to be used. David's brothers questioned his intentions. They accused him of being self-motivated and prideful. Yet, I don't see any of them offering to fight the giant. That's where criticism comes from. It comes from the mouths of those who aren't willing to do what it takes to win, and are angry at those who do.

What others are doing will never fit what you are to do. Don't be afraid to use what has been working for you. Never try to use someone else's equipment. Be yourself! God chose you because there is something about you He is interested in. If He wanted to use Saul's armor, God would have chosen him. Have you been given something that God can use? David had a slingshot. I am certain that thousands of men his age had a slingshot. When you are anointed it will take less to do more.

The proof you are anointed is that you will exude confidence. David's size and stature doesn't intimidate Goliath, it's his confidence that intimidates him. David showed no fear!

Goliath wasn't the door for David; He was a key to the door. Goliath died too easy. Anything that dies easy isn't your problem. Goliath was the instrument to change David's season. He was the only way a poor shepherd boy could find access to the palace. The real problem would be how David was going to outlast King Saul.

Get ready God is about to take you to places where you have no history. David had never lived in a palace and thus, had no idea how to act in the palace. Getting in the right place is easy, staying there until you can change, now that's the challenge. Up to now, David had been performing on what he already knew. He's already used his slingshot more than once. But now, he's in a place where he has nothing to base his decisions on. This is where the favor mantle is revealed.

Those who are destined to rule will have to be willing to be in places where they are out of their element. This is where favor makes no sense. David meets Jonathan, who is the King's son. Jonathan is being trained to be king and is in line to be king. David is anointed to be king, but is not trained to be king. Jonathan is trained, but not anointed. David is anointed, but not trained. Yet, you can't rule if you are not trained. God knows the anointing is not enough. The anointing is power to perform miracles… being trained, is the anointing to build people and make right decisions. Favor, is when the trained are willing to train the one who is anointed. Jonathan recognizes the gift in David and is willing to train him to sit where he was supposed to. That is FAVOR!

Get ready to show you are anointed. Stop allowing your pain and problems to keep you from your destiny. God is about to take us where demons fear to tread. Why? Because we are anointed! You have no idea where God would take you if He knew that you would know how to act when you got there. You are one relationship away from anything you want. God is about to send you a Jonathan. Your about to experience a Jonathan connection! Why? Because you are anointed!

Say this right now! THE HARVEST TIME IS NOW! I AM THE HARVEST! HE IS THE LORD OF THE HARVEST! THE HARVEST TIME IS NOW! Did you shout that out loud?

Get ready to sow some of your greatest seeds. Why? Because you are about to experience the greatest harvest yet!

Week Fifty - Two

THE MEANING OF CHRISTMAS

WHATEVER WE DO, LET'S NOT LET THE WORLD TAKE CHRIST OUT OF CHRISTMAS!

No matter whom you are, your heart cannot resist the beauty of an ornamented Christmas tree, or the glow of a mysterious menorah. Cynicism gives way to the celebration when carefully preparing holiday sweets or stringing colorful lights around the entrance of your home. Any heart warms to a rousing rendition of "Joy to the World" or the sensuous smell of roasting chestnuts on a crisp winter's eve...

There is a lot of controversy and confusion in people's minds over Christmas and its meaning, both in our personal lives and in the world.

The Christmas festival emphasizes this shift in two ways; one, is the rebirth of the soul, and the second, is the return of the light to earth   Yet, even knowing the true meaning of the Christmas season is not enough to convince some people of its importance. **"Peace? Goodwill? Humbug!"** they cry, just as Scrooge did in the famous Dickens fable. "These are nice ideas, but no more than a fantasy. I feel no peace. I know no goodwill!"

THE POWER OF CHRISTMAS:

"I have always thought of Christmastime when it comes round, as a good time; a kind, forgiving, charitable time; the only time I know of, in the long calendar of the year, when men and women seem by one consent to open their shut-up hearts freely, and to think of people below them as if they really were fellow passengers to the grave, and not another race of creatures bound on other journeys." ~Charles Dickens

It seems there is an underlining evil that is using people to stop any mention of Christ in our society today. I am incensed at all the media attention given to people wanting us to stop saying "Merry Christmas." I don't believe that the word 'MERRY' is the reason for their objection, however, I do believe, that "Christmas" is the word that is under attack... WHY? Because the word 'Christ' carries power and eventually does damage to the kingdom of Hell.

This is America and America was founded on godly principles and godly ideals. Yet, I'm wondering, what has happened to those ideals?

What is all this fuss really about? It's about doing away with Jesus. Let me encourage you, Christmas will never be erased just because someone stops saying "Merry Christmas" and replaces it with the phrase "Happy Holidays." Christmas, is more than just an annual celebration. Christmas, is the very essence of what keeps this world from self-destruction and from evil conquering the land. For if there hadn't been a baby born named, Jesus, we would all have troubles beyond our wildest imagination.

Let me grind this axe. Why is it always the Christian faith that is under attack and not all the other religions? It's time for CHRISTIANS TO STAND UP AND BE COUNTED! Let's fuss back... take out newspaper ads...write letters to your local Mayor, Senators, Governor, and President. **ATTACK, ATTACK, ATTACK!** I have one thing to say! THIS MEANS WAR! I'm tired of sitting on the sidelines. It's time to get in the game! Let me encourage you... We're not in it to win it, because we've already **WON IT**!

We need to get a game plan. There's one thing I know; the ungodly with a plan, are more powerful than the godly without one. God has given us everything we need to conquer from helmet to silo. We are equipped to do warfare. We are supposed to be soldiers in the army of God, not the weak, not the lazy, not the fearful, but in the army of God!

Are we going to sit down and allow the homosexuals to lead our children into messed up marriages? Are we going to let a 'Tom Cruise' speak more about Scientology than we speak about Jesus? Are we going to let the NAACP rule us! NO!

WHAT CAN I DO?

- First, get on your face and start praying for this nation.
- Second, sow seeds to those who are fighting this issue in Washington, men such as, Pastor Rod Parsley, Pat Robertson, Jay Sekulow and others.
- Third, VOTE in all elections.
- Fourth, open your mouth and be counted. Stand up for what is right! **We have a right to fight!**

If you encounter any hostility, or have questions about your Christian rights, contact the ACLJ at 1-757-226-2489. (Taken right off Jay Sekulow's website)

JESUS IS THE REASON FOR THE SEASON! This still stands in my heart, as I know it does in yours. This Christmas, take the time to reflect with your family about the true meaning of Christmas. Remember, Christmas is more than giving gifts, it's about giving Jesus!

Christmas is so irritating to the enemy because God didn't stop at the manger. He allowed His Son to be crucified and then He raised Him up to pay for our sins. If this baby had lived and died a normal life, there would be no war, no fuss and no opposition. Let this encourage you! All this attack means one thing. **THIS JESUS STUFF IS REAL AND POWERFUL!** Satan knows it.

Let me encourage you to enter this season of Christmas with the intention of being a personal messenger of light and love, and celebrate in the name of service to Jesus our King. Nothing transforms the ordinary into the extraordinary more directly than the intention to do whatever you are doing with *the desire to serve Jesus Christ.*

When we celebrate the season with this intention and desire, we not only experience Christmas . . . we actually become Christmas: an agent of rebirth for the soul and the bringer of light.

Someone, once asked the question, while they were looking at a nativity scene, "Who's the baby in the manger?" The answer to that question is what makes the devil tremble. The Son of God! So go ahead devil, give it your best! No matter what you do, you can't erase what is living and not dead. Jesus is Alive! Thus, everyday, not just in December, **Jesus is the REASON**!

ABOUT THE AUTHOR

Dr. Jerry Grillo's vision is to bring the body of Christ to a greater knowledge of God's love for them and to forge a greater awareness of His desire to bring blessing, increase and victory in every situation they face in today's world.

With this in mind, Dr. Grillo and Pastor Maryann founded Living Word Fellowship in Hickory, North Carolina, in January, 1995. Now called, **The Favor Center**, it is a place of healing, restoration and revitalization for those looking for a God who is more than just a Savior, but Lord in every aspect of life.

Dr. Grillo spent fourteen years in youth ministry after completing his studies from Southeastern College in Lakeland, Florida in 1986. Through circumstances early in his ministry experience, God planted in Dr. Grillo a deep burning to "glean the fields" and "harvest souls" that religion had discarded as unreachable and valueless. This has remained the focal point of his passion in ministry and the driving force of The Favor Center. Since its inception, The Favor Center has brought hope to the community by feeding, clothing and assisting many who are homeless, unemployed, uneducated, hungry and hurting. This is truly the reason Jesus came into the world.

Dr. Grillo holds a Bachelor of Arts in Pastoral Ministry and a Masters in Counseling and Psychology from Christian Bible College and Seminary in Independence, Missouri. Dr. Grillo holds a Doctorate of Divinity from St. Thomas Christian College. He is also a member of AACC (American Association of Christian Counseling).

Dr. Grillo is a life coach and well-known conference and motivational speaker. He has traveled locally and internationally and has authored over twelve books.

Dr. Grillo and Pastor Maryann have been married since 1988 and have a son, Jerry, III, and a daughter, Jordan.

WHAT OTHERS ARE SAYING ABOUT
DR. GRILLO

Dr. Jerry Grillo lives what he teaches. It has been my privilege to be his personal friend for a number of years. He is a living example of a victorious leader. His church is a victorious church. If you can't succeed under this man of God you can't succeed anywhere. His revelation is life's fresh air in a stagnant world. He is one of the happiest and most exciting leaders I have known through my thirty-eight years of world evangelism. It is my privilege to commend any book he has written.

Dr. Mike Murdock
The Wisdom Center, Dallas, TX.

Dr. Jerry Grillo is truly a gift from God to my life. I love his passion, his purity and his painstaking commitment to purpose. It is very obvious that he loves the God he preaches to us about. Should you ever have the privilege of peeking into this life, you would know without a doubt he's one of God's favorite. Bishop Grillo, what a wonderful refreshing, what a wonderful friend!

Pastor Sheryl Brady
Sheryl Brady Ministries
Durham, NC.

Dr. Jerry Grillo has an important message that is simple, direct, and critical for our times. He addresses the most basic issue for the emerging generation, but it is also the crucial message for all ages. It is the message that Jesus came to earth to share with us about the favor of God.

Pastor Rick Joyner
Founder and Senior Pastor
Morning Star Ministries

His broad experience in counseling in the area of human relationships and outstanding leadership abilities are rare to find. I love his pure heart, steady integrity, loyal friendship and his valuable counsel as a trusted board member of Rock Wealth International. I recommend with complete confidence Dr. Jerry A. Grillo. He will certainly be an asset to your life and any organization he associates and works with. Favor will follow you because of your connection to his life! I am honored to call him my friend.

Dr. Todd Coontz
Rock Wealth International

If you have been looking for a shining light to cut through the fog of doubt and shine forth the F.O.G. (Favor of God), you have found it. These series of manuscripts are some of the most powerful teachings on favor that are in the Christian world today. Dr. Jerry Grillo, I believe is one of the premier voices to this generation... Get ready; the chains of doubt, poverty and lack are about to be broken off your life.

Pastor Clint Brown
Faith World Center
Orlando, FL.

Decision Page

May I Invite You to Make Jesus Christ the Lord of Your Life?

The Bible says, *"That if you will confess with your mouth the Lord Jesus, and will believe in your heart that God raised Him from the dead, you will be saved. For with the heart man believes unto righteousness; and with the mouth confession is made for salvation."* Romans 10:9, 10

Pray this prayer with me today:
"Dear Jesus, I believe that You died for me and rose again on the third day. I confess to You that I am a sinner. I need Your love and forgiveness. Come into my life, forgive my sins and give me eternal life. I confess You now as my Lord. Thank You for my salvation! I walk in Your peace and joy from this day forward. Amen!"

[Mail this in to Dr. Grillo]

☐   **Yes, Dr. Grillo! I made a decision to accept Christ as my personal Savior today, and I would like to be placed on your mailing list.**

Name_____

Address_____

City_____

State _____ Zip _____ Phone_____

FOGZONE MINISTRIES
P.O. Box 3707, Hickory N.C. 28603
1-888- FAVOR-ME   www.fogzone.net

FAVORED PARTNERSHIP PLAN

Dear Favored Partner,

God has brought us together... When we get involved with God's plans, He will get involved with our plans. To accomplish any vision it takes partnership... It takes people like you and me coming together to accomplish the plan of God.

WILL YOU BECOME ONE OF MY FAVORED PARTNERS TO HELP CARRY THE BLESSINGS OF GOD ACROSS THIS NATION?

In doing so, there are three major harvests that you are going to experience...

1. *Harvest of Supernatural Favor*
2. *Harvest for Financial Increase*
3. *Harvest for Family Restoration*

Sit down and write the first check by faith, if God doesn't increase you in the next months you are not obligated to sow the rest.

Yes, Dr. Grillo, I want to be one of your monthly partners... I am coming into agreement with you right now for my **THREE MIRACLE HARVESTS.**

> **Thank you,**
> **Dr. Jerry A. Grillo Jr.**

PARTNERSHIP PLAN:

____**300 Favored Champion Partner:** Yes, Dr. Grillo I want to be one of your Favored Champion Partners of $42.00 a month; involving my seed as one of the 300 who helped Gideon conquer the enemy of lack.

____**70 Favored Elders:** Yes, Dr. Grillo I want to be one of you 70 Favored Elders of $100.00 a month. I want to be one of those who will help lift up your arms so that we can win over the enemy of fear and failure.

WE WANT TO HEAR FROM YOU:

Yes, Dr. Grillo I want to become one of God's…

__ FAVORED 300 CHAMPION AT $42.00 A MONTH

__ FAVORED ELDER AT $100.00 A MONTH

__ SOW A ONE TIME SEED FOR $_____

__ *please place me on your Monthly Mailing List.*

…………………………**fill out the form below**……………………

Name_____

Address_____

City _____State_____ Zip_____

Phone _____Email _____

Credit Card # _____

Exp. Date_____ Circle   Amx   Visa   MC   Discover

Mail this in with your check made out to

"FOGZONE MINISTRIES"
P.O. Box 3707 Hickory NC. 28603   Phone 1-888- Favor- Me

Website www.fogzone.net

What You Connect To You Will Eventually Become."

Church Meetings - Multitudes are ministered to in crusades and seminars throughout America in 'The Favor Conferences.' Dr. Grillo's heart is for the Senior Pastors.

Books and Literature – Dr. Grillo has written over twelve books... with over 20 book ideas to be completed. "Daddy God" is given to many around the nation as a seed book.

Prison Ministry - Dr. Grillo's heart is to reach out to those in prisons and to accommodate those who are hurting; he sows all of his books to those in prison and **"Daddy God"** has been given to a majority of Prison Ministries around the nation.

Videos and Tapes – Thousands are listening to Dr. Grillo all over the country, through his videos and tape ministry. He has over 40 series to offer the Body of Christ.

Missionary Ministry –   Dr. Grillo is dedicated to outreach. 'Love Feast' is the outreach ministry of the Favor Center. This ministry, feeds, clothes, and ministers to thousands each year. It is the passion of **Fogzone Ministry** to help build outreach ministries all over the nation.

Television and Radio – The Favor message is being aired all over the nation. Bishop has appeared on **TBN**, **The Harvest Show, Lesea Broadcasting**, **WBTV 49** Augusta GA., **WATV 57** Atlanta GA, **WJZY UPN NETWORK** and so many more. Dr. Grillo's ministry is changing the lives of millions. **"Favor Keys**," seen each week on various stations around the nation is reaching millions.

Dr. Grillo is in great demand. He is anointed to motivate, encourage and coach people to their greatness. If you desire to have Dr. Grillo speak at your next event.

Call, fax, write or email the information below:

Attention Dr. Jerry Grillo
P.O. Box 3707 Hickory, NC. 28603
1- 888-Favor- Me Or 1-877-593-9673
Email Fzm@charter.net
Fax 1-828-325-4877